LOVE
UNFU*kED

Also by **Gary John Bishop**

Unfu*k Yourself

Stop Doing That Sh*t

Do the Work

Wise as Fu*k

LOVE
UNFU*kED

**Getting your relationship
sh!t together**

GARY
JOHN
BISHOP

HarperOne
An Imprint of HarperCollins*Publishers*

HarperCollins books may be purchased for educational, business, or sales promotional use. For information, please email the Special Markets Department at SPsales@harpercollins.com.

FIRST EDITION

Designed by 212 Creative, Spokane, WA

Library of Congress Cataloging-in-Publication Data is available upon request.

ISBN 978-0-06-295231-8
ISBN 978-0-06-324529-7 (Merch. Ed.)

22 23 24 25 26   LSC   10 9 8 7 6 5 4 3 2 1

This book is dedicated to those who can no longer wait for the world to get its shit together and so must step up to the plate themselves. Welcome home.

Gary B

Contents

LOVE
UNFU*kED

1

And Here's What You Could've Won . . .

And Here's What You Could've Won . . .

Admit it.

You want one of those amazing, fulfilling, and profoundly connected relationships, the one you'd read about, heard about, seen, or even dreamed of, don't you? Maybe like the one your parents had or your friend has or the one you saw on TV. Someone who gets you and you get them, and all is good in the world.

We all *want* that relationship. But here's a nice, healthy dose of oven-fresh reality for you:

You don't know shit about having an authentically great relationship.

Sit with that for a moment. Soak it up. Let yourself get smacked around by some logic for a bit here.

Why can't you have it?

Because you've been sold the ideal without ever being taught the hard truths about what it takes to have that kind of relationship. We're going to take a good, long look at those together.

Whether you're twenty or sixty, currently (happily/unhappily) married, or in a partnership, if you're dating or single, perhaps you feel you're unlucky in love, or you've become a radioactive Chuckydoll magnet or maybe you're so soured, so hurt by your past you've become as cold as a well-digger's ass (thanks, Tom Waits, and yes, that rhymes), lonely, suffocated, tired, or lost, I wrote this book for you.

We all know what we ultimately want out of a good relationship, but how do you get it? For most people, it comes down to a lifetime game of "potluck," of hopefully finding "the one"; and even when/if you do, then there's the mystery of keeping the magic alive for long enough to justify your decades-long investment.

Given all of this, you might be jaded about relationships; hell, maybe you're swimming in them or scared to death of them or frustrated or desperate or whatever your story is about you, and love, and being connected with someone—this book is your pathway to something truly fucking great.

And yes, I'm including those of you who *feel* like you're doing pretty damn great at it right now too. This book may well save you a whole bunch of future heartaches.

I'll be talking about a love relationship in the context of marriage here, but you don't need to be married—or even in a relationship, for that matter—to embrace this book and reinvent your story. Whenever I say "married" throughout these pages, insert your situation.

Oh yeah, and if you're about to get married, soak this book up with everything you got and make sure your partner-to-be does too. It will change everything.

But if you came to these pages looking for the solution to the problem of your husband/wife/boyfriend/ girlfriend/bit on the side/top/bottom/partner/lover, you will not find it here. What you will find, at least initially, is the problem of *you* and how that plays out with your significant other. It's not about finding out who is to blame (like that ever solved anything) but rather uncovering all the flawed ways in which *you* operate. When you've worked your way through that little quagmire, we'll finally give you a real structure to start having a great relationship with another.

Relationships Are All Around Us

Be straight with yourself here. Which relationships are a bit of a sore spot in your life right now? Which one just came to mind when I asked the question? Yes, that one too. There's something afoot in those situations that may not be obvious to you. Your entire life is a function of relationships. All of it. Your love life, your career, your hobbies, your pets, your finances, your successes. It's all relationships.

First, you've got your relationship with your parents, both in the past and in the present. And we all know how you relate to that one can fuck you up.

Then there's the relationship with your current or future spouse—how you get along (or don't) will affect you daily for the next ten, twenty, or eighty years, from the moment you wake up in the morning until the moment you kiss (or sulk at) each other good night.

Then there's the relationship with your boss and your co-workers. Are they assholes? Are you an asshole back? Then don't hold your breath for that next promotion.

There's the relationship with your best friend. Oh, the times you've spent together, the laughter, the tears. And then there's your not-so-best friend. And that distant acquaintance you sometimes cross paths with at the gym. What was their name again?

But it doesn't stop there. There's your dentist. Your landlord. The heroic driver that delivers all that shit you order from Amazon.

Then there're the nonhumans. Your dog, your cat, your hamster. The neighbor's dog, the bird that's always in the tree outside your window. You may not talk to them—or at least they don't talk back. But you still have a relationship.

And your relationship network even extends to inanimate objects. You have a relationship with your car, your house, and even your favorite pair of shoes. Here we're using the broader sense of the word "relationship" to indicate a connection between you and the object, place, or even idea.

You're connected to the place where you grew up. You're connected to your go-to comfort food. And many of us, you'll probably agree, are a little too connected to our smartphones.

Your consciousness is a function of all you are *conscious of*, and you have some kind of relationship with everything you are conscious of.

Hell, you have a relationship with me right now, whether you're reading or listening to this. You're thinking, "Hey, I like this guy" or maybe "Ah, what a load of old shit."

Even the relationships we seem to lack are still forms of relationships. You're still in a relationship with your ex, even if you haven't talked to them in years. And if you're single, that's a relationship too. You're related to your mate by your lack of a mate. It's a relationship defined by its absence.

Here's what you have to realize: every element of your life is so filled with relationships that the quality of those relationships dictates the quality of your life. How well they're going is how well you're going, and your ability to empower yourself to be free or in charge of your own hooks and triggers in all of those situations will be key to your success.

And if your story insists you're not good at relationships, well, you're fucked. It's as simple as that.

So here's the coaching—*Get good. Quick.*

What We're in For

I've wanted to write a book about relationships for a very long time, but I knew the timing had to be right. Almost everything I've written until now has been about getting you on some kind of positive trajectory in your life with a fundamental understanding of what makes you tick. If you haven't read those other books, go read them. They're powerful and insightful and will put life power tools in your toolbox, not pencils and paper clips. It doesn't matter in which order you read them, by the way, just fucking read.

What if you could have a real-life blueprint for how your relationships can work in a fulfilling and clear way? What if we could simply cut through the haze of mystery and the clutter of your automatic thoughts and behaviors to put you in charge of how this goes?

Before we get to that, let's clear the air here with a brief summation of what we are NOT going to deal with when tackling this apparently tricky subject:

Will I be giving you tips on communication? Nope. Too surfacy. You're basically trying to get tips on how to handle your own point of view. Shift your view, and communication will shift with it.

Perhaps you'll get some insight into how you can change or cope with your partner? Nope. All about "them." See above.

Maybe you'll see some information about personality types (including all the trendy stuff about narcissists)? Nope. Done to death and inspires a context of setting you up as a victim. While there's *no* shame in admitting you were a victim to something, it's not a viable way to live your life, even as a triumphant one, no matter how much you or others might try to convince you otherwise.

A resource for healing from past traumas? Nope. Can be great work but not for what we are specifically doing here.

A guide to forgiveness? Nope (although I've covered this topic extensively in my other books, so . . . no excuses).

What about fear of commitment or meddling in-laws or family upsets, infidelity (past or present), financial woes, weird (to you) sex, morality disagreements, ethical disconnections, and pretty much everything else that swirls around this genre? No. None of that stuff either, although what you discover might well make a lot of that stuff clearer for you and the pathway to a great connection finally doable.

What *are* we doing here? Great question! We're going to get into *you*, specifically:

* how you do relationships;

* why yours seem to have a certain predictable flavor;

* how all of that plays out in your life;

* and finally and most importantly, how you can completely reinvent yours now and forever.

I'll show you what you need to handle before you get into a relationship (if you're already in one, you get a reboot . . . YAY!), how you need to manage yourself when you are in it, and finally, the ninja elephant in the room, how you end a relationship—which includes those of you who have zero intention of ever doing such a thing.

And what does this book mean for you now?

It means if you want this to work, to *actually* fucking work, you'll have to embrace it all, entirely completely and without second guessing yourself down the rabbit hole. Give this all you got, surrender to something other than your usual shtick, something that may seem scary or complicated or that you simply think won't work in your case. This is not a toes-in-the-pool-and-see-how-it-goes mentality. This is more like a let-all-of-it-go-and-dive-the-fuck-in attitude. Now, this isn't an approach I automatically take with my work. I'm usually a "take your pick and leave" kind of guy, but not this time. That's why you'll need to let this stuff percolate in your brain. Read, take a break, question yourself, unravel your tightly wound attachment to certain ideas, and allow yourself plenty of room to wonder and build and inspire yourself.

But stay true to this all the way through. No exceptions.

This might be the first book of mine you have read, or you may well be settling down to your second, third, or fourth one now, but if you know anything about me and my idea of personal growth and development, you'll know that I often take a counterintuitive approach to things. And this book is no different.

But be in no doubt, this book is absolutely brimming with the critical ingredients to create a real, lasting, and profound connection with another human being. The kind of relationship that's robust and authentic and expressive of who you really are, but of course, you can't have that if you are too attached to some

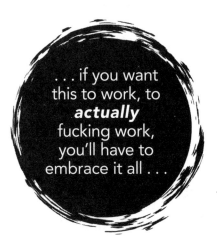

. . . if you want this to work, to **actually** fucking work, you'll have to embrace it all . . .

past you have about how relationships are supposed to be. You just cannot have something new if you're committed to the old. I need you to be bold and inquisitive and courageously open to a different, sometimes disruptive perspective. There'll be plenty of room for your resistance and attachments to the past in these pages too. When (not if) that happens, I have one request. Handle yourself. I won't be spending any time here trying to convince you to reinvent how you do your relationship. That's not my job, that's yours.

You might get inspired; you might get confused or angry or confronted or apathetic or resigned. That's fine; notice how you feel, acknowledge whichever state arises, set it aside, and move the heck on. In short, you need to deal with you in such a way that you can dig a little deeper and expand sufficiently to let something new in.

So where do we go from here? To the bottom. The very bottom, wherein lies the truth. Not someone's version but rather the unmuddied reality of what's going on in your relationship.

2 Telling
Yourself
the Truth

Telling Yourself the Truth

Your only real hope of fixing your situation, of improving your ability to start, maintain, and keep good relationships, is first to acknowledge that your current relationship just doesn't work. That's the crucial first step. You may feel it's okay here, it's fine there, occasionally great to good. Maybe you feel like your situation is in the shit. Either way you need to throw out the old and create the new.

Unfortunately, many of us are like that person who has a slight leak in their tire. Instead of getting it repaired or replaced, like a functional human being, they stop by the gas station every morning on their way to work, put some more air in the tire, and say it's working. In reality, it's "working" just enough to get you to work, silently leaking air with every rotation, every mile. The air is seeping out into the ether, little by little by little. Tomorrow morning or the next or the next, you'll go through the same silly little ritual of refilling that tire, "fixing" it for another day.

, it could easily be solved, finally taken

ou can't even get to that point until you

, admit that what you have, what you're doing, just ain't it. Even if you're making it work, there has to be better than that, surely?

As Kierkegaard once said, "People settle for a level of despair they can tolerate and call it happiness."

It's the same for our relationships. Some of us settle for being lonely, and staying positive, looking on the bright side every now and again, telling ourselves we're happy being single. Or we settle for a relationship that fills our lives with anxiety, heartache, fatigue, or frustration while insisting everything's okay. Fill that fucking tire, baby. One more day. *haha*

But again, our relationships, good or bad, send ripples throughout our whole life.

When you're driving around on that leaky tire, it actually has an effect on you, even if it's not a conscious one. It's another little drain, a microstress, a weight to add to the myriad of other ones occupying your freedom of thought and mental clarity and personal power. In the back of your mind you occasionally wonder if you'll make it to your destination okay, how long the tire will hold out, how you'll afford a replacement, or how you can find the time to get it fixed.

"People settle for a level of despair they can tolerate and call it happiness."

I'll do it tomorrow. . . . Yeah, it's been more than a month now.

Eventually we become so used to this game we're playing that we forget we're playing it in the first place. We build these things into our lives, accommodate them, altering our plans to include them and handle them but never truly deal with them. We forget what it's even like to have a perfectly working car—or in this case, a totally flourishing relationship.

In the words of Fyodor Dostoevsky, "Lying to ourselves is more deeply ingrained than lying to others."

We lie to ourselves. Then we pretend we're not doing that, then the pretense becomes so ingrained we call it reality. We tell ourselves it's working when it's not working. We tell ourselves it's fine when it's not fine.

And this reverberates not only through our own lives but also through the lives of the people we have relationships with.

As the above quote implies, sometimes it's the people that try not to lie to others that lie to themselves constantly. And sometimes we think we're saving a relationship, that we're doing a favor to the people in our lives, by letting less than ideal relationships linger and stagnate. We live the lie. It becomes a way of life. We're solving the problems, dealing with the obstacles, overcoming, overcoming, grinding and shuffling, and trying to make it.

We think if we try to improve the relationship it'll hurt their feelings or lead to a confrontation. But what's actually hurting them—and you—is continuing with this broken, dysfunctional relationship, which leaves both parties worse off.

What I want to talk about is how to make those relationships truly work. Not to simply function without falling apart, not to get you to work without the tire going flat, but to run on all cylinders.

Does that mean happily ever after for you and all involved? No. But that's part of the issue with our lives in general, isn't it? We think it should be going one way when in fact it's going in another entirely. And oh boy, is THAT a problem!

Now, as I mentioned in chapter 1, most of what I'm saying can be applied to all kinds of relationships, but I want to focus on marriage in particular because it is obviously one of the most important relationships in our lives. It has a bigger impact and lasts longer than nearly any other.

And at the same time, in our modern world, marriages are possibly the most dysfunctional relationships. In the United States we get married less, with only 6.5 marriages per 1,000 people. We get married later, with the median age of marriage now 30 for men and 28 for women. And as you've probably heard, divorce rates are at nearly 50 percent. To put that in perspective, there's one divorce every 13 seconds.

"But Gary, it's not so bad. At least 50 percent of marriages are successful!"

Eh, no. Not getting divorced doesn't mean your marriage is successful. Some of those relationships may even be less successful than the people who got divorced on good terms. They could be staying together just to spite each other or to avoid the pain of being judged or exposed or financially ruined.

When I give speeches, people applaud when I tell them I've been married for twenty years. But what are they applauding for? For all they know, my marriage could be terrible. I mean, it's not, but they're applauding a number without knowing anything about the context. Like I'm doing well to have stuck it out this long or something! I've never really been into the long-service medal for a marriage. What about rewards for quality or joy or connection?

My wife and I have been together for more than twenty years. But do she and I actually get along? Do we still love each other? Are we truly happy?

We could be. Or we could be truly stuck. But that automatic desire to applaud the time spent still married seems more like an acknowledgment of tenacity or sticking to something rather than perhaps the real point of being married for that long—that we love one other very much and there's nowhere we'd rather be than in each other's company.

Of course, I'm not saying that it's bad to be married for that long. What I'm saying is that we might need to start setting the bar a little higher if we want to build truly successful, truly rewarding connections rather than rejoicing in what amounts to little more than a long service medal.

We need to stop thinking our relationships "work" because they're not completely falling apart or because we haven't quite killed off each other yet. That's not what a good relationship is.

A good relationship improves and enriches our lives; it's a shared experience but at the same time a very personal one. Can't get your head around the concept of shared *and* personal? You do it all the time. When you go to a restaurant together, watch a move together, or work out together—in fact, whenever you engage with another or others in a social setting, you are sharing the event and experiencing it personally. And that's fundamentally what's going on in a relationship.

But you've got to be willing to work for that experience you're having. And right here there's a shift. I'm a little hesitant to use the word "work" here at all because it's overused and because it sets you up for a dynamic of doing things for reward—I do my bit and you do yours.

The idea of our relationships being "work" plays a big role in the current paradigm of relationships too, one where we use our own "efforts" (and therefore someone's perceived lack) to justify our bad to mediocre relationships. "Well, I did my part."

That's just not good enough. It's another example of pursuing a failed strategy over and over and over until you slide into the blame game and then you're off the hook for how this is going. Off the hook? "It's shit; I've done all I can and they're not playing the game. It's their fault." Poor fucking helpless you. If you're triggered by that, that's how far into the paradigm of blame you've slid. You can only hear these words inside a context of who is at fault.

For starters, there's no relationship points sheet. "Well, I gave her that unexpected little gift, so that's three points." "I organized his/her closet, so that's got to be a five-pointer." You're not building equity. Marriage is not an investment account where you do stuff to grow your worth so you can use it later for a bit of self-indulgence or to get your way. That mode is silly, it's unproductive, and it's also a potential road to ruin.

I get it. I mean, we want it to be fair, right? I do for you so you should do for me! Fine, then you should also learn how to deal with disappointment and unmet expectations with the inevitable disagreements and arguments that arise in their wake.

That whole thing is called a sham, it's not a relationship. It's point scoring and then waiting in judgment to see what the other side does. When the score gets too one-sided? Game over.

Not to mention how we all see life differently; therefore it becomes almost impossible to agree on the score consistently anyway. If your relationship devolves into one of discussing the score line regardless of anything else, that's a pretty fucking low bar.

You cannot quantify the greatest relationship in your life by numbers. Not by percentages, points, or units; none of that stuff. You can't measure this with a calculator, a calendar, or a fucking abacus.

Until you realize that, you'll always be stuck on the ground floor, hopelessly pushing buttons for this thing to go up.

Look closely at your relationship. If it's not working, why? It starts by acknowledging the truth.

Okay, So It's Not Working, Now What?

When I first began telling *myself* the truth (the starting point for every half-decent transformation), I simply wanted the relationship that was *not* the one my parents had. I wanted something deep and influential and connected, but my method for producing such a thing was . . . well . . . fucked. You might have taken the opposite approach from me and attempted to re-create something that was just like the relationship your parents had. Both are doomed to various forms of catastrophe, anywhere on the range from beige to the all-out carnage of a Jackson Pollock masterpiece.

Why is that the case? In the first instance you are using the formula of something that fundamentally did not work as a template for something that you're hoping will. Seems like a good plan on the face of it, right? Eh . . . no. You don't use a failed strategy as the foundation for unparalleled success in this critical area of your life. Whatever you're doing in this life, if your measure of success is "better than catastrophe," you're hardly setting the bar at a level that will allow you to elevate yourself to the wispy echelons of superior fucking enlightenment, are you? Many people haven't even realized that this is in fact their mode in relationship because they're so busy working on the model, they can't see what it's based upon.

The model could be your parents, your friends, something you read in a book . . . you name it, you've probably heard it in one form or another. On TV, from our friends or relatives or wherever, we are all flailing our arms in a thick stew of relationship bullshit, grabbing onto whichever little bread canoe of sense we can find just so we can make it through the goo to the end relatively unscathed.

This could be a moment for you to take stock of what you've made your relationship about. Look at it now, maybe even take a scan back a ways. Reflect. Be honest. —— *love, my happiness, security.*

Maybe this doesn't quite ring your bell, so what about another idea, of using a great relationship as a blueprint? "I mean for fuck's sake, Gary, aspire to some greatness here!"

No. Same shit, different flavor.

You're now completely hooked by how this thing "should be" and "shouldn't be," constantly holding yourself and/or your partner to some iconic ideal, a pressure that for many eventually just becomes too much to bear. Sound like you? If so, open up to some new thinking, let go of your need to justify or explain how your situation is "different" or "unique."

Sometimes that's the problem. We become so fascinated by our own shit, so dripping in the mysteries and the complications, we disregard the simple solution because what is being offered is so painfully freaking obvious that it can't possibly be it!

And it mostly is.

Your partner can never be your mom or dad or ex, no matter how much you might try to make them be that for you. And how could they? It's an impossible ask. They are themselves, and your constant wishing they were someone else chokes off the opportunity for you to create something truly great with them.

A lifetime of denying someone the space to just be who they are will never go well. Particularly the constant stream of clipping, correcting, cajoling, and manipulating masquerading as "helping" or "saving" them.

But what about those partners that are alcoholic or an addict or engaged in one kind of self-destructive behavior or another? You have a call to make. This is either going to be your life or not. I know that's a difficult choice to make but you're currently making one that hasn't proved to be easy already, haven't you? You're still in it. You can only save those people who are open to the idea of being saved and, as harsh as it sounds, sometimes turning your life in another direction is the change that everyone needs, not just you. There's no in between. In or out. But when you say in, you're buying into ALL that "in" means and no, your hopes or dreams or whatever will not save you from the inevitable hardships and tests that are coming your way. I can appreciate you may be drawn like a moth to a flame, that the martyring of your own happiness seems like the right thing to do, but if that's your choice, then own it.

By choosing to be "in," you are also, by default, giving up your right to complain about it. Why? It's your choice, my friend, and if you do not like it, change it.

Your life is a constant stream of your personal choices and decisions, even the ones that you feel you had little or no option but to take. You can either relate to what I'm saying here as good news or bad news, but even that is your choice too.

Identity Relationship

Even though we never admit it to ourselves, we walk into relationships with the desire to find someone who will fix our issues. We all spend our lives overcoming something: a sometimes subtle, sometimes prominent feeling of inadequacy or imperfection, the little hole we just can't ever seem to fill. That predictable, unfillable hole temporarily masked by the hypnotic mirage that the person we're getting into this relationship with might well be the answer we've been looking for.

It isn't always about relationships, either; it's a cycle of self-sabotage that we struggle to break free from. Try it out for yourself. Set a big goal, something life-changing, and then watch how your own internal mechanism will systematically conspire to keep you stuck right where you are. In the day-to-day of your life, it won't seem like that's what happening, but when you step back and look, it most definitely is the case. You'll get hit by doubt or a change of heart or some life obstacle or problem, perhaps overwhelmed by stress or whatever, but it all ultimately leads you back to the same place. Stuck. I covered this notion extensively in my book *Stop Doing That Sh*t*. You're wired to keep yourself in a certain range of everyday life, faced with very predictable problems that you'll spend your lifetime solving again and again. You don't fill the hole because you're not supposed to. You're supposed to just keep trying, grinding up against life until you die.

It's only natural that we'd subconsciously try to fix ourselves by pairing ourselves with another person who seemingly takes care of our own apparent shortcomings, right? But that's only half the story. That's right, it gets worse! What do you think was driving the decisions of your partner when they met *you*? Your eyes or butt? Your glorious smile or captivating conversation? How about your job or bank balance? I mean, maybe some of that shit, but what if they did just what you did? What if they were unconsciously attracted to whatever they saw in you as the answer to their own internal conundrum?

More often than not, all connections are a match made in subconscious heaven. But you might now be starting to understand why they end up feeling like a real-life hell.

Two human beings, hypnotically following what's on the surface, driven toward each other by what's constantly stirring and incomplete in their backgrounds.

I call this phenomenon the "identity relationship," and it is, in my experience, the single most common thing that compels two human beings to connect with one another. Underneath all the usual, everyday explanations of attraction and compatibility and sexuality and Hallmark Christmas movies or convenience there lies another beast altogether.

It's not that they "complete" you, it's more like they fix you. At least initially.

But here's the kicker: this person is also the perfect foil for all those incomplete items from your childhood. They are a focus for your old complaints and upsets and turmoil that you shoved down and regularly get regurgitated in your adult life. It's not that your partner has become your mom or your dad, it's that you only ever engage with your upsets from that perspective.

You know this is true. Think back on your relationships that mattered most. Just beneath the surface of the attraction, there lay your answer. The answer. To you.

We go willingly into our most potent relationship as if we've finally found the answer to the problem of ourselves. The situation where someone else's identity seems to make up for whatever yours needs. Even when there are signs and alarms and people telling us otherwise, we dive in there anyway. Whether it's their confidence or their kindness or their ambition or leadership or popularity or sense of calm, there's undoubtedly the "something" they have that's the answer to the "something" you do not.

We get into our most meaningful relationships as a solution. Eventually, that myopic strategy can become a massive problem. We get in there, lit up like a Christmas tree, thinking we've finally found *the* answer, but eventually this union becomes our biggest problem. And often, getting out of it seems like the only thing you can do. The last and final resort.

Ultimately, what is there for you to think about right now? Let go of the idea that your relationship is flawed or broken or whatever and instead start to open up to the notion that the problem is much more likely your approach to or model for the relationship. Get your nose off the surface and take a deep look into the abyss of what's behind all of this.

You see, if what you get out of relationships is a product of how you take them on, rather than trying to fix or change or improve something that seemingly doesn't work, then all this will take on a new approach. And I mean *new*. Not different, not improved, not refurbished or reinvented or rebuilt but in fact . . . new.

Which brings us back to our point. To create something new, this is about you and what you are doing or not doing.

"But Gary, I don't know what I'm doing wrong."

Okay, now that's a place where we can start. Realize that what you believe and what you tell yourself have real power. And that ultimately your opinion of yourself, of others, of life, of absolutely anything is the first barrier to your producing something genuinely unique and remarkable in any area of your life, not just this one. You'd rather be *right* than have love. We gotta get past that barrier.

3 You Can't
Always
Believe What
You Believe

You Can't Always Believe What You Believe

Remember in chapter 1, I said that the problem was you don't know shit about having an authentically great relationship?

Whoa!!! What!?

Hold your fire there, Eros.

You may agree with this statement, you may disagree, you may feel as if you at least know *something*, all of which are completely irrelevant. Why? Because they are all opinion, and ultimately your opinion of yourself, of others, of life, of absolutely anything, is the first barrier to your producing something genuinely unique and remarkable in any area of your life, not just this one. We mostly seek agreement for our opinions rather than engage with authentically questioning them.

The good news is that you can change your opinions.

But even if we manage that, we may well bump up against the most challenging of all your constructs—what you *believe*. And changing what you believe is a whole other kettle of fish. You see, what you believe is, for you, *the truth*, the granite foundation of how you engage with life, your all-encompassing view. Contrary to popular myth, you are not guided by your view, you are imprisoned by it. And your view is the one thing you'll fight tooth and nail for, even when it's bullshit and destroying your finances, your health, your family, career, or, in this case, your relationship.

You see, at some level it just has to be our way because the alternative would require us to let go of something, some idea or notion that we have held on to for so long, life without it seems unimaginable. This book might then seem like an assault on some of those items for you. And that's okay. But trust me when I say that your addiction to being right about what you believe can be the biggest wrecking ball to what you want, whether you see it or not.

When it comes to relationships, you'd rather have your view over having love.

For some of you I just explained your trail of broken hearts in those eight words. On the other hand, you might be pushing back on them. Do not. Settle in, think about it, and what you'll find is both a personal and a human issue.

You're right about what's right, you're right about yourself, about them, about money and family and who was to blame and on and on and on.

We love being right. Even if it's wrong. Even when it's destroying and disrupting all that we profess to hold dear.

If you take a quick look in the areas of your life where you have serious relationship problems, either with family or friends or the supposed love of your life, either you believe you are right, or they believe they are right. And that belief is the anchor that holds it all in place.

Whether you like it or not, you are the same as everyone else: you'll give it all up to be right, to hang on to what you believe. You'll do it in little ways, you'll do it in big ways. Even when it's costing you life-affirming love and connection. And you'll do it by making the situation you are in okay, by convincing yourself that you're not bothered or that you're fine, or hell, even better off by doing what you're doing. You'll

You're *not* okay, this is *not* fine, you *are* bothered, and this shit needs to change.

gather evidence and agreement and affirmation for your actions but we both know it's all a pile of bullshit because you are getting hooked by what I'm saying right now as you're reading this.

You're *not* okay, this is *not* fine, you *are* bothered, and this shit needs to change.

Being right has a grip, and if you want your life to work, you'll have to ease that grip yourself. We'll get into this phenomenon at various points here, and even if you consider yourself open to change, willing to reconsider what you believe, we'll see how open you really are when your addiction to being right gets exposed and it's sitting on your chest like a three-hundred-pound gorilla wearing a Mandalorian Helmet and singing "Don't You Want Me Baby?" in a fake English accent.

Your problem may well be that you'd rather have the gorilla than the stress of finally dealing with removing it. At least initially.

In the interests of clarity, when something is accurate it has no emotional tag. On the other hand, *being* right is just that, it's a "way of being" and as such it's always weighed heavily with an emotional investment— resentment, anger, judgment, superiority, smugness, it doesn't matter; take your pick. But even now, after I've uncluttered this point, if you're doing some mental acrobatics to declare your current view of your situation as "accurate," that's usually a good sign you're in fact chin-deep committed to being right about it too.

"But I am right!"

Are you even listening right now?

If you scan around your life, this attachment will reveal itself to be much more prevalent, much more destructive than you'd ever imagined. It's everywhere. If you're already coming up with "What about them?" you're gloriously missing the point and the opportunity for self-reflection.

For what it's worth, I have no problem with confronting what I believe or even changing what I believe because I'd rather have happiness and love and passion and adventure than the tattered and bitter token of self-righteousness to console myself with on those cold and isolated nights of my life, and you should too.

It's Not You, It's Me

And now we've hit the heart of it: the problem is you. In other words, you're not "up to" love in your relationship. Then what are you up to?

You might be saying, "Wait, but no, my partner and I just aren't on the same page." Fuck that. Compatibility has become so engrained, we apply it to everything. We're looking to find people and situations that make us feel better rather than getting to the bottom of *ourselves*, to make *ourselves* more robust, more open, more well-rounded. Instead we get stopped, frustrated, can't turn it our way, and boom . . . we're out. Or they are. Same shit, really.

We cut, chop, and dice until we have the perfect little life within which we can live without getting hurt, wounded, or distressed, and if anyone comes along who upsets that fragile mini-verse, CHOP! Out they go. What does all of this mean? It means you get smaller, your world gets smaller, you become more sensitive, more anxious, more worried, and ultimately uninspired. You're a big "being" in this world and you're more than a match for what it has to throw at you. You don't make your surroundings smaller so you can cope with what you have, you do the work on yourself, you grow, you get bigger, more flexible, and more adventurous and develop an appetite for life that only wanes upon your ultimate departure from this mortal coil.

Relationships are critically important, and they are *everywhere*, but that compatibility itch compels us to take people out that we feel don't fit our ideal, all the while never realizing we're making ourselves smaller, more polarized, and more limited.

There's an impact to everything you do, even the things that have good intentions.

Many people seemingly get along, dabbling here, trying it out there, maybe even in some kind of relationship but, at the same time, kinda not. Sound like you? You might be of the independent persuasion, selective of who is in or who is out of your life; you might be someone who feels they can easily go long periods of time wrapped up safely in your self-reliant, impregnable matrix of reality. That makes you not always the easiest person to be married to, unless your partner is the same way; then you can both be alone together. Until the balance gets out of whack. The problem with "independent" as a character trait is that you're always trying to solve your relationship issues on your own. Think about that for a minute and why your strategy is flawed.

It's completely fine for you to live a solitary existence, and many, many people do, but even in that equation you have a relationship to relationships. Is it okay to live the "single life"? Yes! But at the same time, it's all too often the only answer to those who have just suffered too many defeats in their attempts at producing a worthwhile relationship that they love. I get it! Why even bother? And after all that drama and bullshit, it makes total sense that someone would find peace and quiet on their own, but the straight of the matter is, like it or not, we are always related to each other, either positively or negatively, passively or otherwise, AND we have a massive say in how those relationships go.

We often don't feel as if we have all the say, but we do, and I'll show you how. In short terms, if you're looking to change your own behavior so you might see some change in another, that's a mistake.

If that's your aim in all of this, you, my friend, are fucked.

You change yourself to change yourself, and that's it. Often (but not always) a by-product of changing yourself allows other people to see and interact with you differently. I usually look upon that as a bonus.

Your partner, and your relationship with them, is never going to fix your issues and insecurities. Only you can do that. The good news is you have the power to do that, and in doing so, can truly take on reinventing yourself and your relationship.

But . . . but . . . but . . .

Maybe you feel like you're doing the work to change yourself, but also that you're the one doing all the loving in the relationship, it's not reciprocal. That's not how love works, regardless of what you've read or heard. Love is an expression, remember? When you get married, you're saying, "This is the one I choose to love." If you're now in a spot where you are looking to your spouse to fulfill some need in you, that's fine, but you need to be upfront about that. Bear in mind, they might have little or no interest in providing what you think you need in just the way you think you need it.

If that's the case, and what you "need" is now at a critical point, are you willing to walk away from a relationship with someone who is either unwilling or unable to play the game the way you see it?

You can be in a relationship like that, but you finally have to come to terms with your choice. And while I can fully appreciate that you may have complicated circumstances, you either submit yourself to working through your spouse's brand of expression and creating happiness where you are, or you make the change.

As a word of advice, pay particular attention to all the words I am using here. They are articulated in a very deliberate way that is designed to put your hands on the controller of this thing called your life. If you find yourself stopped by or resistant to my choice of words, if you'd rather phrase this in a fashion that defines you as the victim and someone else as the threat or perpetrator, fine—come back when you're ready to dig yourself out of that hole you dug.

When you accept the idea of generating your own experience of being alive, there are always solutions.

When you put that on someone or something else, there are always problems.

On the other side of this coin, what if love wasn't there for you when you started the relationship? What if your relationship was one of convenience, and now you're stuck?

Like everyone else in this equation, I got you too.

Relationships have remained one of life's great mysteries, an unfathomable enigma squeezed into a tempting morsel of idealistic bullshit with only a not-so-healthy side dish of superstition and survival to supposedly help us get through the rough times.

You, like most of us, not only bring your best to your love life, you also bring your worst, including your deeply held fears and your life-learned methods of manipulation to make things go your way. Then there's the way you deal with upset and disagreement. Do you play dirty, get mean or angry when things don't quite go in your direction? Perhaps you get quiet and resentful or try to paper over the cracks with hope or positivity or ignore your problems and issues in the vain hope that they'll simply disappear.

In life there's always the temptation to get your attention on the other person in your relationship, and you'll need to manage that flawed idea here too. I know it's fucking enticing to indulge the thoughts and beliefs and stories that you have about them and what they do and what they shouldn't do and their baggage and their bullshit and their blah de blah, blah fucking blah, but you simply cannot get derailed from what this book is fundamentally centered around.

You.

A word of warning. If you are currently in a relationship that is dominated by physical or verbal abuse, addictions, or any one of a number of undeniable issues, you cannot use this book to fix yourself so it fits into that dynamic. That's not to say this book will not be valuable to you, but you will need to use it in a way that allows you to tackle those things on their own. We do you. That's it. What you do with that afterward is what will have the most telling impact on your relationship.

Do not under any circumstances read this book to try to fix someone else. Do not, for instance, quote this book to your spouse and offer to give them some insight about the shit they need to fix so your relationship with them can improve. That does not work no matter how well intentioned you think you are. You *cannot* fix other people, and you cannot "make" them fix themselves. Period.

"Hey honey, Gary says you're an unbearable asshole and you need to change."

No, I didn't. That was you I was talking about.

By all means talk about what you discover here, share what you got, even buy them a copy, but that's it. It's their choice to read and grow. The truth is personal growth is just that. Personal. The person themselves has to want it, and if they don't, they fucking don't.

Leveraging your threat of leaving won't work here either. Sure they may jump to attention, sure they may even make a change here or there, but ultimately it will only be a façade to keep you happy or off their case. Don't do it.

When it comes down to it, the real problem is that most of us are in relationships to fix ourselves anyway, so buying a relationship book to fix yourself makes sense. When I say "most" I, of course, mean all of us. Whether you agree with this or not is completely irrelevant. You're not buying a fucking book about relationships if you've got this down, are you?

And fixing yourself is just another word for personal development. In broad terms, personal development is the opportunity to develop yourself personally. In most cases it's not about getting rid of old or unwanted behaviors or moods but rather recognizing those in critical moments of life and striking a blow for some new and untested ways of being and acting. To explore all that self has to offer in the day-to-day moments of one's life. That often produces new results in your life and in most if not all areas of your life.

The minute you start using personal development insights to strategize ways to manipulate, change, or shift other people in your life, you're done. That's no longer personal development, and you'd probably be better off learning magic tricks or the art of disguise because you're not the real deal, you're only really interested in forcing things to go your way instead of becoming the kind of human being who can navigate anything and everything.

Life *can* go your way, but not by force or manipulation or strategy. Work on you and it will all fall into place; just let it all go and surrender to yourself. You'll see. When you're finally at peace with you, everything around you becomes much more doable, much more workable and appealing.

In all our lives, we tolerate the busted and the broken, the distant and the numb, and the pained and the strained. I'm not saying people haven't tried, but there's always a point where we just tolerate. We put up with it, or we pretend that we're not putting up with it, like we're over it or that somehow it isn't really bugging us.

It seems that no matter how many times I talk about this, there are always people who are thinking, *Thank God I don't do that anymore.* But the reality is, those folks are as much a part of what I'm saying as those that know they're doing it. That's the problem with tolerating, of putting up with it; we do it for so long we become numb to the effects of what we're doing. We've actually convinced ourselves we're handling it or over it or whatever, while the reality could not be further from the truth.

So if we're up for acknowledging that you won't always be right, and that you are the only person who can change in this relationship, let's get to the next part. It's all about learning how to manage yourself.

4
Taking
On the
Self

Taking On the Self

There's a part of getting into a relationship that nobody ever really thinks of. And that's what we can predictably expect of *ourselves* when we finally settle into the day-to-day of coexisting with another person.

When we start a new relationship, we become so besotted by the future, of our having finally found "the one" (person, situation, or answer), we indulge that rush of emotional hopefulness and plunge right in.

This initial phase is the time when we have gone through the internal arguments about whether we want to be in a relationship versus staying single. Is this person the one for you? Check. You've pondered how this relationship will affect the rest of our life, both positively (definitely) and negatively (somewhat). Check. You've cobbled together a wispy plan in your mind's eye about money and passions and where you'll live, and it's all picture perfect. Check, check, check, check, CHECK!

You can see it all now, this is it, this is the one, this is love, I'm all in, let's goooooooooooooo!

And it's all laid out before you except for the elephant in the room. You.

You've completely ignored the one thing, the one person in the relationship you not only know the best, but that you have full control of: yourself. But you'll be fine, right? I mean, you've found the answer in this other person, so it's all mostly roses from here on out.

Hell, no. No way. And somewhere in the crevices of your thoughts, you know it.

Here's the question you need to ponder: how do you deal with *yourself* in this relationship?

How are you managing your own destructive traits? What have you put in place so you can powerfully manage your own hooks, triggers, and self-sabotaging ways?

Just to be clear, "a few drinks" is not self-management. Neither are "hits" or "tokes," and neither is "retail therapy." Ignore it? Good luck.

Your general reaction to the suggestion of managing yourself can tell you a lot. If you're dismissive or defensive, surprised, curious, or even all-knowing, the message is clear. You are not looking in the right direction when it comes to you and relationships because all of these responses indicate a distinct lack of awareness or ongoing management on your part.

And that's step one to managing yourself: being aware. Being completely aware of all the things you typically do that cause problems in your relationships and continually seeing the new ways that those traits present themselves. You see, most people rarely go beyond the point of explanation when it comes to themselves. The ability to consistently recognize your personal theme music, particularly when it seems like it's someone else's tune you're being irritated by.

On the one hand it's not "you" insofar as we're all wired to observe our relationships and circumstances from the outside. The part that is "you" is your insistence that your observations are the truth without ever really questioning yourself.

But nine times out of ten, we haven't even given it any thought. We're more focused on dealing with the other person than with ourselves.

Because, as we all know, it's always the other person's issues that mess up the relationship, right? If they didn't have such a temper, if they weren't so argumentative or picky or lazy or apathetic, if they were more considerate, more loving, more driven, more like your mom, dad, or favorite author(!), if they were less jealous or less judgmental. Fuck sake, where does this end?! Who cares, right?

Just as long as those assholes change, everything will be hunky-dory. "Right, Gary, right?!"

No, stop being so silly and get real with yourself.

Relationship rule 567—Don't do stuff to get stuff, don't change to get the other person to change. Do what you do simply for the sake of who you get to be. When it comes down to it, it's all self-expression anyway.

We all bring our own destructive tendencies to a relationship, whatever they may be. Of course, some are bigger or smaller than others. Some are more direct or indirect. But we all have them.

And if you're not willing to even acknowledge your own bullshit, let alone deal with it, are you willing to see the undeniable hypocrisy of perpetually pointing to the behavior of your partner?

If your partner is a person (as opposed to a cat, credit card, or a porn channel), they'll have their own shit to deal with and handle. But listen, I get it, it's much easier to see the solving of their problem as the solution to yours. And that's another of those failed strategies.

Until you can, you shouldn't even be in a relationship. Period. Because there's no integrity there. You're looking in ALL the wrong places.

No matter which way you cut it, marriage, and relationships in general, have been about striking up some kind of agreement with another human being. About finding a common ground with agreement to love, to treat each other a certain way, to be faithful and true, and well, you get the picture.

And it's just not working anymore because it omits the one agreement that you never made, the one you didn't even pay any attention to, the biggest deal of all that you'll ever have to make.

The deal with yourself.

I mean come on, you know yourself, right? You know all about your own petty jealousies and upsets, the direction you turn when it doesn't go your way, the moods, the ways you get your revenge or manipulate or dominate situations to get the result you're after, the smatterings of darkness and sabotage and the bullshit that was peppered over every relationship you'd ever had before.

Come now, this is your time. Every great transformation begins with the truth, remember?

So join the dots. Start to see yourself. The whole of you, not just the highlights or the lowlights but the daily you, the one who someone else has to live with. I know, you're fucking great blah de blah, but get your shit into landscape mode here.

Let yourself confront you. By way of inspiration, one of the greatest moments of my pathway to self-realization thus far has been the moment I realized I was the asshole. It was so freeing!! I just finally admitted that as much as life had thrown my way, I was just not the beacon of virtue and light that I had pictured in my head.

The key here is to be able to see yourself fully and accept *that* person without turning it into yet another tragedy or drama. The more you look at yourself, the more you'll see all that shit as something that is, in fact, not you but rather the ways of being and acting you regularly get attached to.

Read that again. And again. And again.

Of course, a relationship still requires you to give your word to someone else, whether spoken or unspoken, and we'll get to that in the next chapter, but if you can't give your word to *yourself*, how the hell can you give it to another person? The foundation of your agreement with anyone should be the one you first made with yourself. An agreement that *you* will manage *you*. A promise.

Are you willing to recognize and handle all the times when you're prone to anger as your default response? Or to realize when you're engaging in another pity party for no reason—and nip it in the bud? Or to stop weaponizing the silent treatment to punish your partner whenever something doesn't go your way? Are you willing to own your propensity for "make wrong," for finding fault, or for blaming too quickly?

How about all those times when you say it "doesn't matter" yet we both know you're stacking that shit away for a day when you'll pull it out to justify yourself or your position?

Are you committed enough to wake yourself up when caught in the trance of your jealousy or moodiness or coldness or wandering eye—or whatever *you* struggle with—for the good of the relationship?

Can you handle your addiction to pointing to circumstances when explaining your own behavior?

If you can't manage yourself, then there's no deal. In fact, without that agreement with yourself, you're not even in a place where you can authentically step to the negotiating table with another.

So what's the deal you need to make with yourself?

A Contract with Yourself

Ponder this golden question for a moment— "Am I willing to diligently manage myself and my commitments?"

The answer to this is absolutely critical in the reinvention of your relationship. If you cannot get yourself lined up with what this is asking of you, you are dealing with the relationship equivalent of a constitutional crisis, and all the "yeah, buts" and "what abouts" in the world will not save you from the white-light glare of what we are exposing here.

Are you willing, are you open, to *consistently* and powerfully manage yourself and all of your foibles and to do it in a way that allows you to stay on top of *yourself*?

No matter the situation, no matter your circumstances, the question still stands, and if the answer is yes, you move in one direction; if no, you have to face some facts. Even if the answer is temporarily "no," at the very least you are confronting your basic unwillingness to be the unifying source of your relationship.

However, take a genuine look at you and what you say you are committed to. Let me walk you through what this question is asking of you and, ultimately, what you are asking of yourself.

The two most important words in this question are:

* *Willing*—disposed or consenting; inclined. In other words, are you *open to* and *agreeing to* managing yourself and your commitments?

* *Diligently*—with conscientious and persistent effort and attention. Are you saying you'll stay open to managing yourself and your commitments *reliably* and *persistently*?

This is not saying that you have to be perfect. I'm not telling you to stifle all of your emotions, to turn yourself into a robot or a doormat. We all have our idiosyncrasies, our moments of weakness. Everyone can seem annoying or hard to deal with from time to time. Can you live by those commitments of yours and hold yourself to them? Can you live by what you said when confronted by how you feel?

The key thing here is, if and when you fall back into one of those normal destructive habits or routines, you need to be willing to clean it up. Are you willing to fix situations you screw up, to deal with the messes you make, to soothe pains that have damaged your relationship?

Can you handle apologizing?

"But what about them?!"

When your attention goes to the other person and what they "should" be doing, you automatically ignore *you* and what *you're* standing for. Neither you nor I can make anyone do what we want them to. You either accept them for who they are, all that they are, or you do not, and *if* you do not, go back and ask yourself the golden question.

"Am I willing to diligently manage myself and my commitments?"

All too often you could remedy any disconnect in your relationship by simply stopping what you're doing and possibly reversing course. Maybe it's giving more time or attention to your commitments— or giving your partner some much-needed space when they do not act in a way you think they should.

Even your attempt to grow your connection doesn't need to be perfect. You might still say the wrong things. And it's certainly possible that your actions aren't forgiven or forgotten immediately.

What's important is that you're willing to realize when you're falling into one of those patterns and to make an honest and concerted effort to correct course.

Or are you more interested in being right?

We've all been in those situations. We're at odds with someone in our life—whether it's a partner, a parent, a friend, or a colleague—and at some point we realize deep down that we're the ones who are wrong. We misspoke, misjudged, overreacted, or otherwise made a mistake. We were being childish, cruel, or just assholes. Sometimes it's over something big; and sometimes it's quite petty.

But though the situation is common, most of us, most of the time, do what? We double down. We refuse to admit that we're headed in the wrong direction, even if it's only partially, and often we're even able to convince ourselves that we should stay on this course.

In fact, the more someone engages in this cycle throughout their lives, the less able they are to consciously intervene with it. Eventually they become so deluded that they actually think they're always right, and even clear, substantial evidence that they're wrong isn't enough to convince them otherwise.

Chances are, we've all encountered this type of behavior at some point in our lives.

Is that pleasant to deal with? Of course not.

This isn't a recipe for strong, healthy relationships. Instead, it gets you mired in tense, hostile relationships that aren't beneficial to you or anyone else. And it eventually leads you to becoming a miserable, lonely person, whether that loneliness is physical and actual or simply a product of your mind, where you've completely cut yourself off from other people through your attitude.

This is why you need to manage yourself.

Because if you don't, not only will your relationships be less fruitful in the short term, but you're also just going to continue spiraling down this hole and digging yourself deeper and deeper. The more you let those negative habits and tendencies run wild, the stronger they become and the harder they are to break.

So you have to stay on top of it. Diligently.

In a way, your relationships demand the kind of attention your garden does, or your plants do.

You can stay on top of the garden, watering and weeding, planting and harvesting. Or you can let it fall into neglect. You can have a green thumb or the procrastinating hand of death.

The more you take care of the garden, the stronger and more beautiful and more fruitful it becomes. Even when problems pop up, they're less of an issue. Because the larger and healthier the plant, the less susceptible it is to weeds, bugs, or disease.

But the opposite is also true. The less you take care of it, the more weeds you get. And the bigger and thicker those weeds grow, the harder they are to grab and pull out. And meantime, they're choking out the other plants, stealing their nutrients, taking up space, and obstructing the beauty of the flowers.

A lot of people love the idea of that garden but can't handle the life of a gardener.

And it's the same in our relationships. We love the idea of the good parts of being in a relationship, the companionship, the vacations, the support, the romance and power of it all but start to check out when things get hard. If we don't stay on top of them, they become more and more overgrown. And they become harder and harder to recover, little by little sliding into something we had never quite planned for as we pour in more effort for less positive results. Until we give up with little more than an occasional glance at what once was.

However, the more diligent we are to maintain them, the more we create and expand and explore, the more beautiful and resilient they become, bringing us more fruit in return for our focus.

Who do you want to be in your life and in your relationship? Make a deal with yourself to be that person, then manage whatever triggers or self-sabotaging patterns you need to. Managing ourselves also means becoming the kind of person whose word means something. Who takes promises seriously, to themselves and to others, and lives out of the place of keeping that promise.

If managing ourselves will bring more fruitful relationships, I think that's something we all can sign up for, yes?

5

Can
You
Feel It?

Can You Feel It?

What is your relationship based on right now? Give it some thought for a moment. What I'm speaking of here are the foundations. The ground under your feet. The thing or things that either do or did keep this solid for you. What are you relying on?

Trust? Faith? What about love or honor?

Let's say it's trust. What specifically are you depending on when someone says "Trust me"? Their word.

You are relying on *their* word. Whatever else you might think you are relying on, if you dig a little deeper, you'll see your confidence is being placed upon who they are as a matter of what they said. When their actions match what they say, your sense of confidence is sky-high. When it deviates from what they said, even by a smidgen, you get a little (or a lot) unsettled.

The same goes with love and partnership and loyalty and whatever else you may throw into the mix. You are completely dependent upon the other person behaving in a way that's consistent with what they say. And that's not just true of your intimate relationships but also with all of your relationships.

You assume that people will act in a way that you've either agreed they will or expect they will based on past behaviors or cultural/familial ideals. But here's the rub. Haven't you ever wondered about the magnetic north of *their* compass? What are *they* relying on when they tell you to trust *them*? What do they turn to when that trust they told you about is called into question?

Their integrity? Their moral fortitude? Their self-discipline or sense of personal ethics? Their faith or religious upbringing? How about their sense of right or wrong?

Give me a freaking break!! Now who is the one being idealistic?!

History is littered with apparently upstanding human beings, those that had made an important social status or significant reputation out of their character or professed virtue who found themselves painfully exposed when their once impregnable force field of authority dissolved like a sheet of cheap toilet paper in a puddle. It was abandoned in their moment of testing for something a little baser.

No matter what you come up with here, none of it really explains what all people are ultimately banking on whenever they might be tested.

Let me cut to the heart of this monster. The problem is that everyone does the exact same thing. Instead of using established truths to guide them, they turn to how they feel in the moment. Why do you think people call it a "moment of weakness"? It's the moment when the feelings they *usually* rely upon desert them, so they follow whatever their skin bag of bones compels them to follow right there and then. Just like you too.

To lay the bleached bones of it out here for all to see, it's basically this: you are relying on what they say and do while *they* are ultimately relying on how they feel.

And vice versa.

Why is that such a problem? It's actually a massive shift in the way we do relationships, and we have never addressed that shift.

Back in the day, you relied upon what your partner said, just like now, but here's the kicker . . . so did they. The importance of what they said to you was just as significant (maybe even more so) to them as it was to whichever ears their words fell upon. The gravity of words was final. Now, of course, it wasn't all rosy and perfect back then either, but nonetheless the dynamic was decidedly different from the one we wrestle with nowadays. Don't mistake what I'm saying here as some kind of homage to the "good old days" because there were no "good old days." We've improved dramatically in so many ways and the world is now a much safer, more prosperous, and healthier place than, say, three hundred years ago, but we can certainly look back to those times to mine for the kind of gems that could empower us in dealing with the complications of a modern life.

One of those gems is our relationship to what we say. In the average person's life that relationship is generally downright pathetic because we have lost touch with the power of language.

The exception to this is any place in your life where you are enjoying some kind of success. In those areas your words and your actions get along pretty well.

Look at the rest, though, and what you'll see is a declining ability to state your own truths (which has now turned into an opportunity to complain), of declaring your own dreams and goals, and then getting to work on the real work of personal development.

And this real work involves getting to know yourself as someone more powerful than your feelings. Remember, I'm not referring to *what* you say in this instance but rather how you *relate* to what you say, both to yourself and others. You do not behave like your words have substance. You constantly say things and then never do them. You don't have any power because your words don't, and that all comes down to a loose or weakened relationship between you and your words. You are as strong as the power of your promises. In all areas of your life.

Weak words, weak you. Period.

On the other hand, can you even imagine a life where you did what you said and what you said was big enough to inspire you?

Then your limit is only ever defined by what you declare. Then your words matter more than anything.

And right there you also have the reason why all the moral gumption, determination, or willpower in the world will not save you until you finally confront your relationship to such a thing. Your morality will not save you until you start to see that the real power lies in your personal *connection* to morality rather than the morality itself.

It's the same with a vow. Or a promise or virtue or ethics. Or a contract. Or . . . well, you get the picture. But we'll cover vows more in the next chapter.

It's important to be aware of how often feelings are driving your actions, and to stop letting them do so. The power of your words and your promises, to yourself and your partner, is what really matters here. Live by that and you'll see your relationship transformed.

Arguing

While we're on the power of words and language, let me give you my general rule of thumb when it comes to arguing. Disagreeing and arguing are often viewed as complete no-nos in those popular magazine/ TV/social media constructs, a view that I couldn't distance myself from any farther if I relocated to a two-bedroom igloo on the back end of a Neptune glacier.

Think of your life like a conversational blanket and every time you speak you are weaving the colors and contours of that blanket. You (and your emotional state) continually rise and fall in the day-to-day of your conversations.

Basically, if you automatically talk shit, you'll automatically feel like shit.

"So talk happy, then be happy . . . right?" No.

That's a plastic and surfacy approach to what I'm saying. In your everyday conversations, if you take stock and notice, your mood is connected to your talk. It gets interrupted by occasional triggers, yes, but even they are products of your internal talk.

So, what about arguments? Well, they're a conversation too, and if left to spiral, can become a way of life. That's why I use the 90–10 formula. Show some gumption and keep your arguing to no more than 10 percent of your overall conversations with your partner. If that seems way more optimistic than you're capable of producing, give this some thought. How many conversations do you have with your partner? No really, look at your average day from when you get up to when you go to bed. How much of that is actual conversation? Think of all the seconds and minutes added up. I did some extensive research on this thing (yes, fucking Google, like all you other "researchers" out there), and while the studies vary, it's relatively common to find evidence of your average human being spending an hour to three hours per day talking, and of that, how much is with your spouse or partner? Even if it's (generously) half the time, that means you are in actual conversation with them for thirty minutes to ninety minutes per day.

Fine, you can argue for a maximum of nine minutes a day. Any more than that and you're milking it.

If that still seems like a hill too far, your look in the mirror needs to be a deep and penetrating one. If it's already more than that, reel it in. Argue your fucking heart out and then let it go.

If this seems ridiculous to you, it is. But so is your addiction to being an argumentative asshole, so choose. Instead of focusing on the pettiness of what I'm saying, ask yourself this question: what have you done in your relationship that has created an environment where we have to talk about putting a time limit on your arguments? Of course, this includes your distractions, childhood drama sulks, and pretend busyness that you indulge your bullshit with.

Like most people, you're interested in how to stop or change a behavior rather than how to invent a new one. You're more interested in stopping the arguments than starting the fucking love because you live with the mistaken belief that if you first repair something, you can then switch your attention to something new, something better. That includes the notion that things will only ever work if old shit is fixed. That's a failed approach.

If the cake is shit, you change the ingredients next time you bake. You don't spend your time trawling through your old chemistry notes trying to work out how to make a bag of salt taste sweeter.

Stuff gets salty when you throw a couple of handfuls into your mixing bowl. Changing the kind of salt you use, shifting when you add the salt, only using salt on Tuesday or Sundays or holidays, and on and on and on.

Stop!

It's fucking salt!!

If you want the cake to taste different, either use a lot less salt or up the sugar.

For fuck's sake, I'm exhausted by this analogy. More love, less arguing. You get what you put in. There you go.

And while I know this may seem too simplistic, too naive, or lacking in that magic "something" for you, ultimately what you're staring at here is the heart of your upsets in life. You have a choice. Every day you are presented with situations that while I can appreciate seem to you like there's no alternative but to react, I can very much assure you, there are options on the table.

It seems like we've become a veritable bath bomb of feelings throughout our lives, but none more so than in our marriages. All too often, when that internal spark is "gone," we're gone too.

We're looking internally for a signal; we notice it in little ways, a dash of apathy or resignation, those little piles of irks and annoyances and irritations, the ways they now speak to you (or don't) or the things they do (or don't), the growing case you have been building in your head that gets provoked and stirs into life.

But the truth of it is, we DO have powerful feelings, our emotions DO matter, but where we keep getting fucked up is the degree to which we attach the weight of the universe to them.

You are a significance machine, constantly adding gravitas where there is none and more where there is some.

They forgot your birthday. What could that mean? Add your significance here.

They haven't said "I love you" for a while. What does that mean? Go ahead, add to the pile.

They're more interested in X than you? Keep digging, keep adding; every little bit helps!

Except it doesn't. It slowly destroys.

The truth is not a fucking feeling, and it's the truth whether you feel like it is or not. That's why it's important that you understand and connect YOURSELF with what your particular "truth" is.

You do not have to be guided by your feelings. There's a larger truth that can guide you and your relationships. And I think you'll find that when you're guided by this truth, you'll feel much more fulfilled. Except maybe you don't know *what* truth your relationship is guided by. We're going to uncover that next.

6 You Don't Know Your Vows from a Hole in the Ground

You Don't Know Your Vows from a Hole in the Ground

Just about every marriage ceremony in the world, of every faith, culture, and philosophy, includes some kind of vow, either explicit or implied. I made a vow when I got married, I was even teary-eyed when standing there in front of our families. It was a nervy, magical moment and, just like you, I had no idea of what the hell I was actually doing. I don't mean in the sense of getting married but rather that vow part of the ceremony.

I played my part in putting together this wonderful occasion. I was madly in love and lust and passion. The vow stuff was important, but just for the big day, right? It was ceremonial, but what did it mean in the days, weeks, months, and years that followed that magical day?

When you got married did you realize you were making a public declaration? Did it occur to you that this was your commitment to your partner, your family, your community, to the universe? When those words fell out of your mouth, were you conscious of devoting the rest of your life to whatever you said?

For richer or poorer, in sickness and health, to have, hold, love, cherish, and all that other stuff, till death do you part. You get the picture.

Were you aware that whatever words you said were supposed to now be your mission in life? Probably not.

You most likely did your "bit" like I did my "bit." That part in the proceedings when you "say" your vows and then we get to the next bit and then we're done! Happily ever after . . . or not. And that's how it is for most people.

Let's look at how the dictionary defines vow:

* a solemn promise, pledge, or personal commitment;

* to pledge or resolve solemnly to do;

* to dedicate or devote.

Does that sound like what you signed on to when you said your cute little vows at your wedding? Was that what was going through my mind in my teary-eyed vows? Probably not.

I mean, there's no real point to a vow anymore when you think about it. It's fluff and air and tradition but ultimately fucking useless, AND it was deliberately designed to be a fundamental part of a marriage.

Are you seeing the problem yet?

You see, once upon a time that vow had a whole other kind of significance. Just like how in the previous chapter we discussed how our word, our promises, used to mean something more, used to guide us more than our feelings and emotions, and the vow was a big part of that. It used to be a very important public declaration, a statement made in front of your community, a spoken covenant (a contract!) about who you were and what you could now be counted on for. The use of the word "vow" in this thing was no coincidence. It was serious shit, and the entire ceremony was centered around it.

That vow was the glue, and when you made one, people took notice as it was, for all intents and purposes, your word. Your say in the matter and, in a time when many could neither read nor write, your "word" was your bond. It was how you were related to and known as. That's why gossip back then was far more damaging than we can even imagine now. A person's standing could be undone, and with it their reputation; their job or other source of income; their relationships with others; but, most significantly, their honor.

When that happened, their word could no longer be relied upon. And they were ruined.

Because words fucking mattered! Or more accurately, *your* word mattered.

A vow was, of course, the thing that people would use to cement the deal in marriages. It was the terms and conditions of the union, its raison d'être, the whole fucking point of the thing!!

And now it's not.

That cornerstone of the way that a marriage is designed is woefully out of sync with these times and it's use is completely bankrupt because there is no place in modern language for a vow anymore. No one vows anything! It's not a living part of our conversational domain. It's basically a dead word to us and about as useful as a "forsooth" or "gadzooks" or "hither." All great words, but society is no longer using them in everyday language. They don't mean anything to us.

So by losing the power of the vow, what does this mean for our marriages? Given what I've been laying out here, it's not good, and it really starts to make sense why. The entire construct of marriage is based on an inauthenticity, a falsehood. We have lost the gravitas, the meaning, the weight, and the importance of what was once the most important piece of marriage—what we vowed to each other.

We've kept the vow in theory but we don't use it the way it was intended anymore. It no longer has any substance. Its power is gone, and it has been replaced by a knockoff, low-calorie, easy-on-the-ear substitution.

Is it any wonder why we struggle so much with the notion of marriage and, by default, relationships in general? There's no "skin" in the game. If marriage is *supposed* to be the part where it all gets real, where we finally take our partnership seriously (remember that word "solemn"?), what does that say about our temporary flings and long-term partnerships?

Of course, there are a large number of people who are in committed relationships, some for many years, and who have never married. Some of those may have an intention to do so at some point, but similarly, a significant number have no intention of doing such a thing at all. You may be one of those folks. Join the dots here because, believe it or not, the exact same principles apply to your situation. You are operating out of some real or implied set of promises to each other and, like the people that are formally married, you're either being guided by and living by them or not.

The power of a vow, whether stated or not, is that it gives us something concrete for us to check in and see how we're doing. Without it, or without taking it seriously, there's nothing tangible to ground ourselves with, no framework for us to keep creating from. We're guided by little more than bursts of positivity, nostalgia, and rubbing against the ebb and flow of emotions, moods, and feelings.

But it doesn't have to be that way. We can let our vows define how we live out our relationships daily. We can create a better relationship from the foundation of those words. But first we need to figure out what our relationship is actually about.

What Is Your Marriage Really About?

So, if not based on vows, what is a marriage (and partnership in general) based on now? Well, initially it's based on hope for the future and the burgeoning connection we experienced in the early stages of our relationship, some combination of love or friendship or passion or physical attraction or compatibility. Eventually all of that melts into the background and is slowly replaced with our internal state—how we feel from day to day to day.

Imagine living your life organized around your "word" these days. Many people believe that they do this (at least to some extent), but it doesn't take much scratching at the surface to see that they, in fact, do not. Not at all. How you feel is a far bigger deciding factor in how you react, how you navigate not only your relationship but also your career, your body, your finances—in fact, the whole freaking enchilada, than many of us would like to admit.

Now you can see why it's much more like a roller coaster than a pathway.

But what if we had our personal "true north"? A firm commitment to be someone (or *something*) of our own creation? How would that play out? How could you even manage such a thing? Questions, questions, questions. We'll get to that, but let's first look at the existing status.

What exactly is your marriage based on right now? Think. Right now. What is your marriage based on?

Most of us don't know. We haven't rigorously thought about it enough. Certainly not beyond the mediocre or immediate problems or concerns we have, so the foundation of your marriage, the day-to-day of it, ends up coming down to something like "getting along" or "making it work." The bar becomes so low that the most mundane of victories seems like a typhoon of relief. The reality of our lives is eventually a lot closer to a seesaw of emotional triggers, old incompletions, and a steady stream of Band-Aids in the form of vacations, a new house, different friends . . . basically anything we can muster to interrupt the same old, same old of the relationship.

All too often when a marriage is failing, it gets explained away as a lack of communication or commitment, a drifting apart or the terminal: falling out of love. People do not fall out of love. It degrades from a lack of use, and while you might think that is their problem and not yours, these pages may well cause you to think again.

Many people feel like they've no alternative but to either replace their relationship with something better, or distract themselves with something else so they can live in the pretense of happiness than having the real deal. The noise in your head of "doing it for the kids' sake" or to "avoid the embarrassment" or whatever your reasoning may be, never really placates the slow demise of your self-expression and joy.

Now, maybe you're thinking, *Ha! I knew marriage was old-fashioned. It's simply an outdated institution that doesn't apply to our modern sensibilities.*

No.

As I said earlier, you're in the same boat even if you haven't "taken the plunge" or "tied the knot." Because while the vow may be less explicit, it's still there. There's still a sort of implied contract—an agreement, if you will.

When you and your partner decided to become exclusive, you might not have said, ". . . and that means you don't sleep with anyone else," Why? Because that's universally accepted as a given, it's understood that when you're in, you're in, and that's it. That's the unwritten and often unspoken contract of being in a monogamous relationship. It's the basic level of commitment required to form some kind of workable condition. And there are other unspoken commitments too.

While we're here, I know that some people feel as if the answer to their relationship issues is some form of "open relationship." For varying reasons, the statistical success of those arrangements is acknowledged as particularly volatile. Studies suggest that open and polyamorous relationships have a significantly higher risk of collapse than monogamous ones. There's a failure rate north of 90 percent in some studies, so it's pretty safe to say I'm not going to suggest this as a viable route for you. If you do see this as feasible for you, fine, go ahead, but be aware of those numbers and the pitfalls as you make your way forward.

I fully encourage and empower people to live the life of *their* choice as long as it's with a "no harm to others" approach. Be responsible for your impact. At the same time, whatever path you choose, get as aware as possible of what this path will demand from you, what it will bring in terms of problems and unwanted and unseen changes. How can you see the unseen? You often can't, but at least you can live in the knowledge that it exists, and it may well come your way too.

Whichever route you prefer, there are always expectations, some obvious, some not so, from both parties on how they'll be treated. For instance, you probably expect your partner to be a little more diligent in returning your calls or texts than the random guy you unsuccessfully tried to buy a Ninja blender from on Craigslist.

You probably expect some basic level of affection and attention from your partner, for them to think of you and act in a way that shows you how important you are to them. Perhaps they'll buy you a gift or two on your birthday, put your shoes away for you, make you a cup of coffee, or surprise you with that thing you'd said you wanted or liked. A plethora of unspoken yet often expected items that we sometimes take for granted.

Maybe your idea of attention is just to be left the hell alone from time to time.

These are unwritten rules that we usually don't even think about, but they're there. What they are exactly may change a little from culture to culture and generation to generation, but we all have these relationship presuppositions, whether we acknowledge them or not.

And they're all linked back to that vow, in both married (spoken) and nonmarried (mostly unspoken) relationships. It's just taken up a notch and formalized when we walk down the aisle and officially say "I do."

Except now, that marriage vow has become entirely ceremonial. Outside the event itself, it's not something we feel bound by, if we even acknowledge it in the first place. There's no real and tangible connection to the vow. How do I know that? Well, for fuck's sake, are you awake? Look at your own life. Are you guided by "love, honor, and cherish" (or whatever it was) when you wake up in the morning? How real are your vows in your day-to-day life?

So figure out what you want your marriage to be about. Write it down if you have to. Then live by that. Simple as that.

Who Has the Power?

When we are living by feelings, not truths, or by vague understandings, not vows, all too often our relationship devolves into persistent occasions of disagreement fueled by the desire to be right about this thing or that. It's not the items that you're disagreeing about that is the problem, even though it sometimes desperately seems like it is. It's that you're both dug in *about* them.

Those promises that guided you in your calmest, most reasonable moments don't have the same power in times of stress or upset or apathy. Consider the idea that you're cashing it all in for the emotional charge, the rush of domination, of being the one who has the high ground. The power.

And again, it doesn't matter how you do it. You could be the loud one, the argumentative one, or the one sitting in quiet resentment. Almost simultaneously enjoying your time of self-righteousness while somewhere, in the back of your mind, knowing this shit just does not work. Let those moments in right now. Get present to that familiar feeling and your default way of handling your relationship whenever you're pressed.

Often, when the relationship starts to become an everyday drain on your aliveness, even if it's for a series of things that are minor or temporary, we say fuck it. I'm out of here, sometimes literally, sometimes physically, sometimes emotionally or mentally but, the result is the same. We're no longer in it the way we used to be. In the escapism of your mind, maybe you'll find someone better. Someone who cares, a better fit, the real deal, the "one." How many people are currently drifting along in their current relationship with their mind perpetually drifting off in search of the next one? Dunno, but I bet it's a fucking lot.

You've heard the phrase "one foot in, one foot out"? For some of you, the reality is that both feet are in, but your behavior is coming from the idea that you're *not* fully in this. You have to deal with your relationship every day of your life, the life that you've made with this other person, but somewhere in the crevices of your mind you're holding back—in one minute, out the next, playing the game, taking yourself out of it, on and on, same old shit occasionally interrupted by a half-decent night of sex or entertainment or a family tragedy that temporarily wakes you up or some influx of "feel good" news like a promotion or an unexpected windfall to bring you temporarily closer together, but all of that just papers over the deep and unsatisfying cracks produced by your unworkable approach to being related to another.

Who cares, right? We "make it work" to the extent that we feel like it, and then ride out the rest.

In fact, the person who has the most power in modern relationships is often the one who's more willing to completely flaunt their obligations, who's more willing to do what they want without any thought of promises or vows. It seems that the person who's most willing to end the relationship is the person who's most in control of the relationship.

What a fucking horrible way to be connected to another. It's a life of threat. Where the looming specter of terminating the relationship, of dominating a way of life, is used by one party to control, subvert, and manipulate the other.

Needless to say, this isn't a recipe for a successful, long-lasting love life.

Control comes from fear, so it's little surprise that people would put up the shutters on their vulnerability and turn their relationship into a strategy for survival rather than some kind of lifelong self-expression. What a waste of a life.

If you are in this kind of relationship, either as the perpetrator or the receiver of this approach, this shit has to end. It may be time for some tough conversations but that's just how that goes.

Even if we do acknowledge and live by our vows, we'll find some way to justify breaking them. "Well, they didn't hold up their end, so why should I?" It's not truly binding. It's just lip service, not a real promise.

I can already hear your internal noise screaming as you're reading these words.

IT'S NOT THAT SIMPLE!!

BUT MY PARTNER IS . . . (insert whichever way you say they are here)

HOW AM I SUPPOSED TO DEAL WITH . . . (insert circumstance here)

WHAT KIND OF IDEALISTIC NONSENSE IS THIS???!!!

Whatever your resistance, can it. At least for the moment.

What you're bumping up against here is you, not this book. Even if you're as cool as a cucumber right now, your moment will come. In any case, for many of you this is where you may notice some of your automatic reactions and assumptions, but you may also start to get an insight into the ways in which they are running you. It's your job not only to notice your predictable triggers but also to set them aside for enough time for you to think, to interrupt the mass of thoughts and physical responses to let yourself address another view, a different logic.

I can appreciate that it isn't always easy to do. You, like me and everyone else, are biological. There's a certain chemical makeup we each have that runs in sync with repeated neuronal patterns, which is all a fancy way of saying you are a set of triggers just waiting to happen.

And when they go, you go. But you don't get to throw your arms in the air here and proclaim, "It's just the way I am." That's a bullshit excuse to get you off the hook for dealing with yourself. Every now and again I give people little snippets of the kind of language they should stop using. This one would be near the top of my "don't say it" list.

Think about it: in your day-to-day relationships, how often do you make decisions based on these vows you made to your partner? You might feel compelled to do something because it's a "nice" thing to do or the "right" thing to do or you think you "should."

But we rarely, if ever, come back to the vow. "I promised to cherish her, so that's what I'm going to do. It doesn't matter how I feel about it or how much they're annoying me today." How much simpler things would be if we could find a way to do such a thing. To let go and return ourselves to something more satisfying, more nurturing and real.

"I vowed to stick it out until the end, and that's that." We'd have to make it work. There'd be no question about it. You wouldn't have to weigh the pros and cons or ask your friends for advice.

You *can* live that way, and it would revolutionize your relationship. Try it out.

7
Adding
Value

Adding Value

What is guiding you? (And no, I don't mean some idealistic thing or even a spiritual or religious one either.) What is keeping you within the lines of the life you have? What's the internal influence that distinguishes one thing from another, good from bad, right from wrong, how you should behave, act, or respond? What's setting out the parameters of why you do what you do?

The quick answer that you'll hear from most people is some version of their upbringing or past, usually a dramatized, romanticized, or demonized edition. That is to say, we mostly explain our inner compass in terms of how we were raised. You either reflect the rules of your childhood or you've organized yourself in reaction to those rules, but the theme is the same. (This is very distinct from the subconscious machinery that we all wrestle with that I laid out in *Stop Doing That Sh*t*.)

What I'm pointing to is your personal rulebook, some set of values, an invisible internal compass, and being sure it includes a sense of what's right or wrong, but it's actually far greater than that.

What are your rules? And by that, I mean specifically, what are your values? Before you jump straight in with "faith" or "family," hold your horses right where you are.

Almost everyone barfs up an auto-response answer like that, but if you look at the reality of their life, they're actually consumed by a bunch of stuff such as not talking to their dad, being completely jealous of their sister/neighbor/workmate, plotting misery on their "haters," and hiding a life with more sordid little details than all the episodes of *Real Housewives* combined.

You might be pressed a little (or a lot) by what I'm saying here. "Yeah!! Who the heck are you to judge? You're just some guy who writes books; you don't know what it's like for people, what they're dealing with, what they've been through!!"

Well, first, I'm people too so . . . there's that. Second, you're missing the point while you frivolously indulge your ever-bulging bag of preciousness.

We talked about keeping our word to ourselves and to others, and navigating our relationships from stated vows, but where do those words come from? The words are established from the things we *value*. Now dig deeper. If you set aside the usual kind of reaction one has when asked about their values, when you reflect on your life, what do you see there? What kind of personal values are evident from the life you are living?

See anything?

What about now?

Go on. Whenever you're ready . . .

Okay, fine.

Most likely right now you're either drawing a blank or trying to come up with something. Even if you do come up with something, I'm willing to bet you do not manage diligently or reliably whatever came to mind, and that's because nobody actually lives a life that's truly based on their specific values, no matter what they might say or think. You see, to do such a thing would require you to keep what you value *in mind*—to continually live your life mindfully and to be rigorously guided by all that you value. To be shaped and organized around your own conscious set of principles.

Why is that important? Because we are, by and large, being blown around by life, surrendering to whichever deviant wind gusts our way, consumed by the idea that we have no say, no direction, and all we can really hope for is an eventful turn in the fucking weather.

And that's just not accurate; far from it. You CAN be guided; you DO have a say. and it's incumbent upon you to work this shit out for yourself. And those values can guide the quality of your relationships too.

The funny thing is that we talk about values; sometimes we even talk about them a lot. Some of us tell everyone we come across about them. We, of course, argue about them and post on social media about how important they are, but often we're doing that without even realizing what we're talking about is, in fact, our core values.

"The most important thing in life is . . ."; "we've got to fight for . . ."; and "I'm dedicated to . . ."

Many people make the mistake of unconsciously connecting their values to a cause, which gets them disastrously confused to the point where the cause becomes absolutely everything. The cause takes over, even when the cause itself occasionally or regularly conflicts with their values.

Politicians (across the board) spend a lot of their time, money, and resources working out how to get their agendas to connect with your values to the point where you cannot tell the difference between the two. Often you'll even unknowingly abandon your values to go all in with the cause because the swirl of emotional fervor is so entrancing, so seemingly right and justified and seductive, you lose sight of who you are at one level or another.

And whenever you abandon your values, in whichever area of life you are not aligned with your core, you're off-balance. You're neither settled nor at peace.

The world is filled with people who have completely relinquished their values to a cause. But no matter how noble, right, or justified it might seem, that's no way to live your life. You'll lose yourself.

And it's not just politics. Every day your values are being seduced and abducted in the name of whomever wants to use them to their advantage. But before you start off on some fake ass crusade about being dominated or manipulated, this is on you. Until you start taking some ownership of you, of your own feelings, and taking the time in your life to apply some simple logic, you'll always be little more than a pawn in someone's else's chess game.

That doesn't make *them* bad, it makes you irresponsible, and if that's the path you're choosing, then fine, at least your choice is yours. If not . . . wakey, wakey. You're only malleable because you haven't confronted the cost of such a thing. It takes something to be someone, and all that juice has to come from you. Period.

And nowhere is this sellout of "self" more obvious than in our relationships. Instead of being guided by something a little more concrete in our relationships, we're swimming in this mystery soup of moods and emotions, from love to lust to jealousy and heartache and apathy and everything in between.

We're affectionate when we want affection. We're cold or indifferent when we don't. We call our wife/ husband/partner when we're in the mood to talk. We ignore their calls when we're not. We're honest when it's convenient. And we lie or pretend when it's beneficial. Check in with yourself here, look at your own life, start to see the degree to which you are caught in the same trap as everyone else, coming up with the same old answers to the same old problems.

But real values are different. You bring them from the background of your life, you shine a light on them and apply them to what you are dealing with. You handle what they demand of you, and you step forward into that demand.

How You Got 'Em

There's an old line of thought in philosophy that insists our values are inherited, that you have no say in them, you got what you got, and that's that. That they were instilled in you by your parents, by your teachers, by your surroundings, by your culture, by your DNA, whether individually or all at the same time. The values you hold are simply the ones you've been conditioned to, often without even knowing it.

Because we do unknowingly pick up certain values throughout life. And they're often ones which, when brought out into the unforgiving light of observation, we're not particularly enamored by.

Again, we don't think that's the case. We mostly believe our values are based on something like a robust education, maybe even a rigorous appraisal of the facts, and a logical or moral conclusion about what we should value.

We're not like those other idiots who learned their values from TV or movies. We're certainly not like those selfish assholes whose only real value of concern is that of self-interest.

The problem is, if you ask the average person to explain their values, they struggle because we lazily buy into the socially acceptable explanation of values rather than really diving in to rigorously question our own personal standards. In other words, our values are rarely as well thought out and defined as we would like to think they are. And you know what's even rarer? Actually living our lives by the values we say we are so fond of.

In fact, our values are often in some very real conflict with a number of the actions we take from day to day. Here's a little something for you to ponder, particularly if you are questioning the importance of values in your life. Anywhere in your life you are unhappy, out of balance, out of sync, call it what you will, you are following a pathway that is clashing with your values, and no, you don't even need to know what your fundamental values are to begin to see this.

For instance, let's say I ask you what you value. And you tell me, "Adventure, Gary, is what makes life worth living. That's what I value." Now, I won't deny that adventure is a pretty cool thing to value, and a lot of people would agree with how you feel. Also, designing your life around adventure doesn't necessarily mean you need to start plowing off the edge of a Swiss mountain in a wing suit while wrestling a fucking bear for your new YouTube channel.

It can simply come down to pushing back your comfort zones, trying new kinds of food or books, or taking up hiking or cycling or painting or opening yourself up to other possibilities in your life. In short, for you to think, plan, and behave in a way that's consistent with someone who values adventure in their life.

And yes, you're still allowed to use the toilet, lay on the sofa, scroll through your Insta and whichever other mundane, everyday things we spend our time doing, but the point remains. Your commitment to a life of your values would be unmistakable, even from a distance.

And yet, truth be told, if you were to really sit down and start looking over your life, you'd realize, "Well, actually, over here, I don't seem to be living a life of adventure." In fact, you might see that some areas of your life, when examined from this perspective, are completely about predictability or survival or something else entirely. That would be an area of conflict, where someone is just not living true to who they are.

In other cases, you're not only living in a way that conflicts with your values but that in fact suffocates and suppresses the very idea of them.

Is it any wonder we get so off course and become so fucking unhappy?!

Of course, maybe adventure isn't your thing, but the idea here is undeniable. Maybe you think integrity is more important. Or passion. Or accomplishment. Or self-expression. Or love.

Either way, once you take stock of those values and compare them to your everyday life, you'll start to see all these little places where you're not actually living from them. You value passion, but you have cashed in your values for whatever bullshit you thought would get you by in this life.

You say you value partnership, but you've succumbed to the illusion of control and driven people away from you. When was the last time you let go of that irritating, driving need for things to go your way in favor of a real and satisfying connection with another? You may value self-expression, yet you're shutting other people down. Oh, so it's okay for you to be yourself, but God forbid that that same principle might apply to others.

Most people would say that they hold love as a value. But let's a take a deeper look. You see, if you were actually someone who lived your life like love was a value of yours, something that was a force, a straight line in a landscape of confusion and layers of ideologies and philosophies, you would regularly check in with your values as a standard, as something to line up against your life to handle whatever predicament you were being presented with. There'd be little room for resentment or revenge or anger or frustration because, in light of this new awareness and conscious choice, you'd be drawn back to what is the very essence of your existence: love.

It's not like you wouldn't *feel* those things from time to time (you most likely would), there may even be an overwhelming temptation or monkey brain addiction to indulge your most base reactions. But in those moments, those decisive times, your commitment to your values would arise to clear the horizon, to take over, and to set your course. In those moments, you are provided with the insight you need to settle the situation down. With a little work, your life and your values would align.

And on you'd go. Seems easy, right? Well, it's fucking not.

There's a different group of philosophers who say, no, you do not necessarily have to live by a set of "conditioned" values but instead can invent and continue doing this, reinvent values to live your life by. We can sit down, create an entire set of new values, and then follow them; and each time we do, we are redirecting the trajectory of our lives. We are being guided by a different set of life ingredients, which ultimately takes us to new, challenging, and often exciting results.

Now, I happen to agree with these wily old philosophers who engender freedom of choice. But the truth is, it takes a rather big leap to go from hypnotically following whatever values we've picked up throughout life to the effort of consciously establishing a set of values that will actually help us through the day-to-day, down-in-the-trenches of our existence.

So if we already have a set of inherent values, why the hell do we need to create a whole new set? The main reason is that we do not consistently live by our values, but even more obviously, the kind of values you will need to make your relationship work may not exactly make for the most loving and inspiring connection!

For instance, when I looked at this for myself it became increasingly obvious that I had ended up with certain life values that I wasn't particularly fond of but were ultimately very useful in certain situations although, I might add, completely at odds with my life in others. The one that always springs to mind is "hard work." I value hard work. I inherited this one, and it had become a sacred cow for me. The problem was it was also a bit of a burden too. Time off for vacation seemed like a treasonous act. I felt guilty about relaxation or the prospect of making money without effort. It also played havoc with my marriage, as you might imagine.

Here's some truth for you to sit with. By and large, people aren't guided by their supposed values in nearly any area of their life. Others might apply the value in this or that area while abandoning it in another area.

So how do you start living by your real values? How do you start applying them to every area of your life, not just one or two?

Well, those are big questions and maybe even the kind of challenge you would like to invest yourself in at some point. But remember, this is specifically about your relationship.

It's easy to become distant from what we say we value; we can all too easily disconnect if we do not manage our *commitment* to our values.

Keep that word "commitment" in mind as we move forward.

Your values will make little difference in your life until they become full-on commitments, which is why they need to be alive for you. A breathing, shifting statement of who you are and what you can be relied on for.

But first let's identify what exactly we value in our relationships and how to live by that.

The Value in Relationship

So, what about you and relationships? I mean, look closely. What are the things you say a relationship *should* be about? What lights your fire, settles your demons, and pulls you forward? What is this thing, this lifelong union of relatedness, supposed to be organized around?

Now obviously I'm asking you to set your partner aside here. I'm asking you to let your current situation just "be there" without turning your attention to it or even being influenced by it. Take a swim in the waters of possibility, allow their cooling ripples to wash and replenish your thoughts.

What are the fundamental things you believe are critical to a great relationship?

Love? Connection? Loyalty? What about those gnarly little fun nuggets of adventure or inspiration or hell, a healthy dose of mystery or romance? What are the components that you say a relationship *should* be?

Grab a pencil or pen and start writing down your thoughts. We're looking for a list of one-word values like the ones in the paragraph above.

Again, none of this is to fix your current situation but rather to allow you to start looking at life from a state of what is *possible* rather than what has *been*. Allow your thoughts to flow through this process. If, for example, passion is on your list, what would your relationship look like if passion were a foundational piece? What would you be willing to let go of to have passion in your life?

Now, if you're like most people, whatever you are imagining right now is fairly idealistic, or you might even be bumping against all the reasons why it can't happen for you.

First, this has to be real for you. You must begin to put together a picture of what you would now be doing and not doing in your relationship when you are being true to your relationship values. Second, like anything else in life, if you have become so addicted to why things cannot happen for you, you will always be fighting an uphill battle. I'm not asking you to "believe," I'm not asking you to be positive or hopeful. What I'm saying is, there are two pathways you can follow. One is the pathway of what's possible and the other is one of what's not possible. Both are equal in their availability but distinctly different in their outcomes. Ultimately you get to choose which one is for you.

As I said before, many people can name a relationship value, but all too often what they are talking about is what they would like to see from their partner. Stuff such as loyalty and honesty and communication, but what they're really saying is, "Don't cheat on me, don't lie to me, and when we have problems, talk to me."

Here's what I'd like you to consider as you are putting your relationship values together: you're mostly thinking of things that would either prevent shit from the past happening again OR the kind of values that will somehow take care of your current laundry list of brokenness.

"But Gary, what about trust?"

If you need to introduce trust as a value to a relationship, you are already in deep doo-doo.

Trust should already be there, and if it's not, it needs to be handled like an emergency breakdown. You don't get into a relationship with someone you do not trust. Period. If it has been damaged in some way, get that shit sorted now, get to the heart of why it's not there and what needs to be said and done to ensure it is back in place without delay.

Believe it or not, this is all resolved in a conversation. You need to talk and talk and talk this out until you are both at the very bottom of the issue and there is nothing more to be said about it from either of you. It cannot, cannot, CANNOT be allowed to hang around endlessly toxifying anything good you are both doing. It has to be handled as quickly as humanly possible.

This process may include arguing, crying, snot, sleepless nights, and whatever else the process throws at you, but you both keep going until the item has no more juice. Then, and only then, do you declare the issue complete.

When you declare something complete, you are both agreeing that this item cannot be used in future as leverage for a shitty mood or behavior. It is done as a matter of both your word.

When it's done, it's done. The end of it.

I should add that persistent breakdowns in trust is unworkable. Face the truth and act accordingly.

Next, we are about to take a life-altering turn in the traditional way that we view and participate in relationships. Those all-consuming notions of what your relationship should be are nothing inherently new, right? We all have some picture in our mind of how this thing is supposed to go. In fact, that's sometimes the problem. There's often a cavernous divide between the "how it should be" that you've created in your mind and the ice-cold reality of how it actually is in your house.

All of your arguments, disagreements, and stony silences exist in the no-man's-land between these two worlds.

You see, all of this is a product of one thing. We've been conditioned to see partnership as an equal share. We've unilaterally adopted the idea that we do one thing, our partner reciprocates, they do some other thing, we reciprocate, and on and on and on. But no one has an answer to the giant flaw in this strategy. What if they don't react to what we do? What if we don't "get" where they're coming from and their "move" goes flying over our head?

You need to become some kind of coffee-slurping psychic lawyer, spending your days flipping between mind reading and mounting a firm defense of your case just to work your way through the various stages of discontent in your marriage with this model.

Oh yeah, and then your friends and family are the jury that you plead your case to. And in the final summation, you're the judge.

It's a bankrupt pattern. It doesn't fucking work; in percentages, 50/50 is bullshit here. Why? Because the best you can hope for at any one time is 50! And God forbid they put in only 20 or 30 of their "share"! We both know what happens then . . . yeah, that's right, you put in only 20 or 30 too. And down the spiral we go. Now, of course, this is true in the logic of the agreement, but the most damaging aspect is what this turns you both into. You see, the nature of this particular union is observation. You have to be in a constant state of checking in to see what the score is, who owes whom, who's ahead or sticking to the "partnership" in a way that's fair or right.

How can you be all in when you're regularly on the outside checking the scores?

So what's the alternative?

Simple. It's all on you. You own the entire thing, what it's about, where it's headed, how it feels, how it goes . . . all of it, every last drop, every speck, morsel, atom, and nugget. It's yours.

Let that sink in. This relationship, in its entirety, is on you. Only you.

You see, if you are out to have a relationship that is consistent with *your* relationship values, then it's your job to fucking bring it! Pause here and give this some real thought.

That's mainly when relationships go to hell. We look to "get" from relationships when in fact that's the completely wrong approach. *There's nothing to get!* There's only the opportunity for you to think and behave in a way that's consistent with your values! That's the biggest thing you'll have to let go of—that you'll ever get *anything* in return.

If you do what you do with what you'll get in return on your mind, that's called a strategy. You'll also know your strategy is filled with traps and dead ends that often lead to more upset than they're worth. Give-to-get is basically a bullshit, failed method for trying to manipulate your situation in your favor. It produces self-made victims and resentful assholes in their millions.

But there's another thing. Probably the most critical thing of all.

The thing that fucks people up most about what I'm suggesting here is the mistaken idea that they will be giving their all to the other person with little more than hope that it will somehow make its way back to base. It's not that at all.

You're not demonstrating your values to the other. Why? Because there are in fact three parties in your relationship. There's you. There's your partner. Then finally there's the relationship.

Get this. Everything you do is in service of the third party. The relationship. Ultimately it's what will nourish everyone involved, including you. The relationship part of this trio is what requires your attention, devotion, and loyalty, and right here you'll really need to wrap your head around this.

How will this even work?

Your partner—They can handle their own shit. It's completely their job to make themselves happy, content, fulfilled, etc. They are not your job or your life's work. If they ask for your support, awesome. If you are in a place to give it, give it all you have. If they want advice or insight or whatever . . . also fine. It's still not your job, though. None of this means you do not love them or care for them or want the absolute best for them. You can have both. You can adore that human being all the way down to very last wisp of their morning breath, but their happiness is theirs to express and be responsible for.

When you take responsibility for keeping them happy, you'll pay. And vice versa.

You—You should always be working on yourself, especially on your ability to deal with yourself when you're at your worst. It's a lifelong commitment and one that produces results time and again. You are not their job either. You can make requests of them, maybe things you'd like support with. They'll say yes or no. Either way you'll manage. Be bigger than your feelings.

Side note—Do not ask your partner to make changes to themselves for you. Decline their requests for you to change for them too. That doesn't mean you do not look to make yourself a better human being, it only means ALL lasting and significant change has to come from the person themselves.

The relationship—When it comes to the importance of having a great relationship, this item will demand almost all of your effort and attention. This is where you are reliably bringing your relationship values out to play. If the value is love, be loving. If it's passion, be passionate. If it's understanding, take the time to bring understanding to your relationship.

Every action you take is in service of "the relationship." The dates, the things you do day in and day out, the vacations or gifts all the way down to chores or treats or favors, it's all in service of making your connection deeper and more meaningful, and each of these can be a conscious and deliberate reflection of your relationship values.

When your eye is on the quality of your connection, the connection thrives. Period.

I said we were going to completely reinvent what it is to be in a relationship with another person. And it starts with stating what values we want our relationship to operate from. What are yours?

It then requires evolving those values into a commitment, rather than something you pay lip service to. So let's do it.

8

All In
or Nothing
at All

All In or Nothing at All

By now you might have your relationship values all hashed out, neatly listed in impeccable cursive that you artistically etched with a crisply sharpened pencil on your best sheet of hand-made English cotton notepaper, gently sweetened by the soft smell of walnut and linseed oil. And there it sits, occupying center stage on your quiet, aging leather writing pad that sits proudly upon your reproduction Edwardian desk for all the world to witness its existential glory.

You may be already profoundly connected to these new values, maybe even moved by the possibility of them, and if so, you can see how this whole thing plays out, so off you go with your good self into the future we ride! HURRAH!

Not quite, Don Quixote.

You see, even if they're just scrawled into your hot sauce dabbled napkin with a purple crayon or perhaps still swirling in your head, shrouded in a dash of mystery or confusion or resistance, there's an important part of this puzzle you are ignoring in your hope-addled brain.

Because somewhere down the path of your future the cold light of day will hit, as it always does, not just with you but also with everyone else, and in that moment you'll lapse. Then you'll lapse again and then again and then . . . back to square one.

Why is that? Because while you might well be inspired by the values you are revealing here, the problem is you have no real commitment to any of it. Not really. It's little more than a glorified, drunk-on-hope New Year's resolution at this point, and we all know how those go, right?

You might be enthused, or hell, maybe even lit up by the prospect of the future and what you can bring to the table, but there's something still missing, something you can count on when you get down to the nitty-gritty of life. A kind of relationship glue that will ground you and point you in the right direction when life gets a bit swirly, as you and I both know it will.

You're going to need some personal skin in the game you are about to play. After all you are, by default, a blame machine. When life gets shitty (and it does), you go looking for who is at fault, which gets you off track from what this relationship is supposed to be about. It cannot be about love, for example, if you're resenting someone for their participation, because when that stuff happens, it's now about resentment. Or anger. Or whatever else you might get yourself derailed by from time to time.

You see, whatever dark spot you get yourself wrapped up in, whatever bad mood or automatic reaction or response you stumble into, THAT'S what your relationship is about at those times. Even if it's for a minute or an hour or a day, you should be left in no doubt, in all of those moments, that you are, consciously or otherwise, committing yourself to something corrosive. Something that is undoing what say you are out to build.

Therefore, those values of yours are no good on their own because they are up against some pretty strong views and opinions and old wounds and stress. They just cannot withstand the pressures of life. You'll eventually bend to the path of least resistance, to the easy way out, and the voice of reason in your head will very quickly become the voice of reasons.

Which means they *must* somehow become full-blooded commitments. A conscious and all-encompassing tool that you regularly remind yourself of, align yourself with, and then boldly act from their honesty. Even when you don't feel like it. Maybe even more so at those times.

"Alrighty, then William fucking Wallace, how?"

First, your relationship values have to inspire you. The must call you to a greater good. You'll need to engage your big, giant brain with your big, giant heart until they are singing in harmony with one another.

Your relationship has to rise above your biology, like a beacon of truth, a creation you made in your more sober and reflective moments of calm and consideration. You make a commitment to be guided by these values, and that commitment must begin to lead your life as a sort of personal compass in the area of your most important relationship.

In an effort to be fully transparent here, I'm not suggesting that anything I've said thus far will be easy for you, because in all likelihood it will not. We're inventing a whole new approach, but it is one that works. And, of course, we secretly want to succumb to our emotions, we covertly long for the easier route, to be guided by some automatic, internal, all-knowing principal tied to our ancient DNA or spirit or soul or whatever, the kind of thing that will work all this shit out for us in our moments of need, but contrary to a lot of self-helpy, wishy-washy, pop-science stuff about intuition that's currently gurgling in the back of our collective throats, that's just not how we work.

At all.

While we're here, I'm not a fan of "go with your gut" and couldn't give a flying one whether this ties in with your personal philosophy either. For the "intuition" folks out there, start tracking and taking note of all the times your feelings about something or someone have been flat out wrong.

What about the times you were right? Even a broken clock is right twice a day.

You can no longer buy yourself off with, "We just don't get along," as if there's no choice for either party in the matter. Another common sentiment is something like "They're always getting on my last nerve." In other words, it's entirely the other person's fault that the relationship isn't working.

Second, rather than focusing on external, environmental, and circumstantial issues, you have to turn to managing yourself and your commitments. Remember chapter 4? If you need to go back and get a refresher on what it looks like to manage yourself, I'll wait. Because that's the only thing you can control.

If you say you're committing yourself to love but you get triggered by the same things as before, that's your decision. It's a choice to let those outside factors, like the actions of others, make you go against your values.

When it comes to managing yourself, I'm specifically talking about managing how you choose to respond to people. There's a sort of stoic sensibility here in that, even if you're dealing with what appears to be the most annoying person in the world, you still get to decide whether you're going to be annoyed. If your mother-in-law is nasty toward you, you can be nasty back, you can be hurt, or you can do nothing. You can even choose to return her nastiness with pleasantness or understanding. Just remember, you've never walked in her shoes, you haven't lived her childhood or seen what she has seen or felt what she has felt.

And the same goes for all of your relationships. Now, some people are going to point to extreme situations involving relationships that are incredibly toxic or outright abusive. And you should definitely have a line in the sand where you say enough is enough.

But that doesn't change the fact that you have a choice in how you respond.

There's a crossroads that you come to. And it's not some kind of deep, existential thing. It's a decision you make in that particular moment of that particular day, a fork in the road where you can either go left, or you can go right.

In one direction, you've got the old path, the one you've traveled down so many times in the past. It's familiar, it's easy. What that path is exactly, depends on you. Maybe you tend to react to conflict defensively. Maybe you go on the attack. Maybe you become sad and withdrawn. And just like you drive to work or school each day without even thinking about which road to take, you can often find yourself retracing your steps again and again without a second thought.

But these choices are a big fucking deal, both in our life and in our relationships. They control where we're going and how we get there. And they happen multiple times every day.

That's why you have to recognize that no, you're not on a one-way, single-lane street. There is a fork in the road. And it's possible to take the other path. Rather than getting angry over the same shit, you can choose not to. Rather than falling into the same habits, you can choose something different.

And when you overcome that urge and make the right decision, it's not only satisfying, it's also liberating.

Because not only are you creating a better life for yourself, one that's more in line with your values, you're actually in control. You're no longer just running around the same track on autopilot. You're in the driver's seat.

Of course, it can be tough to take that right turn.

And this is where those values come in. Because it's these moments when we have to be guided by something greater, something that's sufficiently motivating us. We need a "why" if we're going to forgo the momentary ease of choosing the road well traveled, and take the new path, the unfamiliar path leads somewhere we've never been before.

Either you're going to continue indulging in your past or deal with yourself so that you can live a better relationship. It's that simple.

You make that choice instant by instant, day by day.

Dancing with Yourself

But let's change the language around how we talk about relationships: this isn't a battle. It's not a fight. You're not in a ring or an octagon or a dark alley, exhausting yourself as you slug it out with your destructive tendencies. Instead, I like to frame it as a dance. Rather than throwing a punch, it's more like a sidestep. Instead of a kick, you're doing a spin.

That doesn't mean it's easy. If you've ever seen a professional dancer, you know just how much blood, sweat, and tears went into getting that final performance just right. The distinction is that it's more about footwork, grace, timing, and finesse than brute force.

Choosing to dance with your situation, realizing everything you're dealing with is part of a much bigger game, allows you to step back, to breathe, and to let go of the angst of control and having it all go your way. Patience over being driven, speaking over silence or shouting, thinking over the immediate charge of reaction.

However, as counterintuitive as it might sound, you're not dancing with another person. No, not even in the context of a relationship, even a romantic one. You're dancing with yourself. Believe it or not, all great relationships require you to do that.

Think about ballroom-style dance. Unless the dancers are totally in sync, they'll never put on a great performance. But one partner can't focus on how the other partner might mess up. Maybe the partner is off rhythm. Maybe they don't dip at the right time or catch cleanly. Maybe they won't stop stepping on their foot. Even so, the only thing each partner can do is focus on their own performance. That's the only thing in their control.

So you've got to stop looking at your relationships like you have any control over what the other person does or says. You're dancing with yourself, and all you can focus on is your own steps.

"Yeah, Gary, but what about those times when my partner . . ." Yep, those are the moments I'm talking about, when people spin out extreme examples.

However, I've found that what people mostly do is hitch their wagon behind worst-case scenarios to justify themselves and avoid what I'm saying.

What about physical harm?

What about being controlled?

What about sexual abuse?

What about, what about, what about . . .

Look at your real life. Are any of these things present in your relationship? If so, I've already covered this in the first chapter. You know what to do. It is important to be safe and smart.

However, for most people, this stuff is NOT in their relationship, but what they're really looking for is some strategy where they can continue doing what they're doing, everything will change, and bingo! It works!!

No. It. Fucking. Doesn't.

You want change? Change. Commit to your values, to changing your actions, changing your relationship to love and forgiveness, accepting others for who they are. Get committed and buckle in for the ride. If you're not willing to do that—and I mean ALL of it—you're wasting everybody's time, including mine, so put the fucking book down, get a lawyer, and prepare for single life because you're done but you're not willing to own it and take the consequences of where you are. Sure, there are people who stumble into that seemingly perfect pairing and end up in a relationship with someone who just seems to fit them perfectly. But that's not the norm. It's the exception that proves the rule. If you really want to be powerful in relationships, you have to be powerful in managing yourself. Because that's the only thing you truly have control of.

So commit to your values. Commit to your vows. Commit to your relationships. It's that simple.

9 The Deal Breakers

The Deal Breakers

The title of this chapter speaks for itself, right?

These next few pages address an item that is absolutely critical to relationships but isn't discussed anywhere near to the degree that it should be: welcome to your deal breakers.

Now, this is the chapter some of you are going to be giddy about. "Gary, you said this isn't about my partner, it's all about me taking responsibility for my actions in the relationship, but deal breakers are all about the awful things my partner might do!" Don't get your hopes up too high, there. Because this is still about you establishing what you can, and cannot, put up with from another person, and determining what action you will take from there. You still can't control what another person does, only how you respond.

What do I mean by your "deal breakers"? Simply put, these are the things that might happen in the course of a relationship that could have you *considering* if it can continue.

And no, this doesn't contradict the chapters where we discussed making vows and then committing to keep them. If a vow is a kind of spoken contract, then it stands to reason there might be certain things that would cause you to look again at whether you are choosing to continue with what you agreed to.

As we're creating the values that guide how we want our relationships to go, part of those values include how we want to be treated. Becoming a more loving partner doesn't mean becoming a doormat. It means taking agency for your actions and reassessing if things change.

The problem with the idea of deal breaking is that many people feel as if they already know what theirs are. Stuff such as infidelity or stealing or violence or abuse or whatever springs to mind for you when you think of this subject. The problem is, when you're two, three, or twenty years into a marriage and one of these comes up, it may well NO LONGER be a deal breaker for you.

But the goal in this book is that we want to move from the abstract idea of what marriage and relationships are, a vague contract that everybody sort of follows but no one actually sticks to, and into something real, concrete, both in how we relate to it and how we handle it. And that relates to our deal breakers as well.

So how and when do you determine your deal breakers? First things first. You get real about the kinds of things that would call you to question your commitment to the relationship, and you do that without delay. Like right now. What might those things be for you? Maybe that's infidelity. Maybe that's lying. Maybe that's mishandling money. Whatever it is for you, it's important that the deal breaker is laid out as clearly and distinctly as possible. You need to know exactly what it is, and so does your partner. "If you don't show me the level of love that I expect . . ." See, you're already putting in some kind of strategy for manipulation. Because who knows what exactly that level is and how it's going to go up or down depending on the day or your mood?

Let me set you up with an example here: infidelity. Aka cheating, fucking around behind your back, goin' hiking, chexting, unfaithfulness, two-timing, whatever you call it, you know what I mean.

Infidelity is probably the single most common experience that most people would consider to be a deal breaker. It's also one of the leading reasons that people cite for divorcing their spouse or leaving their partner, so it seems like a pretty cut-and-dried affair (sorry), right?

No.

About 40 percent of all marriages will have to deal with this issue but, perhaps surprisingly to many, approximately half of *those* marriages continue after the fling. It kinda proves my point. While people go into their marriage with the idea that infidelity is an absolute no-no, when push comes to shove, people have built lives together, sometimes with children, or businesses, or investments, and a plethora of emotional complications to consider when facing the actual, no-kidding reality of a divorce. When you pile it all up, people often see how much they would be giving up, and the prospect of losing all of this, of letting go, is just too much.

So they stay.

All relationships already have a set of assumed deal breakers, which were never laid out or discussed but are just sort of blithely understood.

For instance, if one partner physically hits the other, that would be a clear deal breaker for most people. Regardless of your opinion of an incident or your judgment or even your (completely irrelevant) explanations, once you get into that realm of physical violence you're very much treading through "it's over" territory. And yet people find themselves sticking around in a situation that would appear to be a complete no-brainer, even when their physical safety is under threat. And no, one time isn't just one time, even if it only happened on a single occasion. The lingering impact of one time or twenty times never goes away.

Stealing is another common example. If your partner steals from you, whether it's your wallet or your purse or your bank account, whether it's twenty dollars or a thousand dollars, you've definitely crossed from the realm of a simple argument or disagreement and often are spiraling down into the realm of "What the hell am I doing in this relationship?"

Until now, everything we've been talking about in previous chapters centered around ourselves, about what you can and can't do personally to build and maintain strong relationships. In fact, I even told you to stop worrying about the external so much and to start focusing on the internal, on what you could directly control.

But let's be clear: that doesn't mean it's not like your partner is not on the line and responsible for their actions. It doesn't mean that they have free rein to waltz in and do whatever they want, whenever they want.

"Well, they pushed Grammy down the stairs, but Gary said I need to dance with myself in relationships."

Not quite. You still need to have some integrity. To be clear about yourself and where you stand.

Most of us are used to the relationship equivalent of those electric fences people use for their dogs. You put a collar on Fido, run an invisible current around the yard, and your poor old pooch figures out where the "fence" is by running until he or she gets shocked.

But your relationship isn't a German shepherd.

You're free to change your mind.

Everyone has their "go to" when their plans get interrupted. Some get determined or defensive or they disconnect or go into analytical overdrive, and all just to shelter themselves from the interruption for the sake of relative safety from some perceived threat or a potentially unstable and uncomfortable future. There's a famous quote by Mike Tyson at the height of his legendary scariness: "Everybody has a plan until they get punched in the mouth." And that's the same thing we're dealing with here, although not with the physical altercation. Everyone has a plan until they get undone by the unexpected. When life steps in and has its way with your dreams.

But it still hurts. And it's still hard as fuck to plan for. And it's even harder to execute that plan when we're still reeling from the impact, when our vision is blurry and we're not sure where we are.

So what are we to do?

Reframe Your Deal Breakers

The point is not to get rid of deal breakers. We just frame them a little differently and, in doing so, make them a little more real.

Instead of a binary yes or no, together or not together system, it's more of a spectrum, one that's activated once that button is pushed or the seal of trust is broken.

Once that situation kicks in, you're reserving the right to question your commitment to the relationship.

And you're not making any guarantees about how it's going to turn out either.

In other words, the result of the deal breaker is not black and white. Rather, setting out your deal breakers is about laying out the field that you're willing to play on. The right side of the field is over here. The left side of the field is over there. And you're letting the person you're in a relationship with know that once the ball drifts off that field, you might not be playing anymore. You might pick up your ball and go home.

If the field gets a little muddy or unkempt, with weeds poking up here or there, you'll push through it. You'll even play through inclement weather, through fatigue or injuries.

But once the ball crosses that sideline, once it goes out of bounds, there's a risk that you call the game at any moment. Especially if the ball rolls out of the stadium and lands on the field next door.

It's about saying, "Look, this might not happen, but I want you to know." And it's just as important, if not more, that you yourself know where the line is too.

But the deal breaker itself can't be a mystery. It can't be ambiguous. That's the fundamental principle that you have to understand. You need to lay it out straight, and you need to lay it out early in the relationship. "What if I'm not comfortable having that conversation?" Then you shouldn't be in a relationship. If you're unable to have these kinds of hard or uncomfortable talks, you're not cut out for a relationship, at least not right now.

It's as simple as that.

"What if they don't accept my deal breaker?" Well then, you saved yourself a lot of time and unnecessary heartache, yeah?

It might take time for people to warm up to the idea of moving in with each other, getting married, having kids, and those kinds of things. But if you're waiting on someone to agree to the idea of not cheating on you, to love you enough to be monogamous when you value monogamy, then you're wasting your time. This isn't a romantic comedy; it's real life.

That being said, this isn't about attacking your partner or throwing them under the bus. Instead, you're mapping out the territory for both your sakes.

So what are your deal breakers? Take a minute to think about what they might be.

After you're clear about what your deal breakers are, start to think of them as something that *changes* the direction of your relationship rather than immediately ends it. Why?

Time.

That gives you the space to think, to process, and to evaluate before committing yourself to a big change. And be left in no doubt, whatever the decision you make, after a deal breaker, EVERYTHING changes, and you need to consider which decision is most aligned with how you want to spend your life. In other words, you need to be fully aware of what the hell you're getting yourself into.

If your ball goes outside the marked lines on the field, it doesn't mean you're definitely out. You can't be sure how you're going to handle the situation in two, ten, or thirty years. But your partner needs to know that if that boundary is crossed, you will do what you need to do to handle your life, whether it's immediately ending the relationship, going into a hiatus, or something else.

By declaring your deal breakers to yourself and your partner, you are declaring the place or places where you will be taking stock of those commitments you made and whether you are open to continuing with them. For those of you who have been bursting to find your "get out of jail" card, this is it, but of course, unlike Monopoly, this release will not come without cost.

You're making it real, both for them and for yourself. And that's ultimately what all of the things I'm showing you are about: making it real.

It's important for us all to think through and communicate deal breakers with our partners. When we allow our values to guide how we manage our deal breakers, we maintain our sense of self and composure and, no matter how tempting and no matter the result, it gives us a place where we can stay clear of the deluge of drama and upset.

10
Breaking Up to Get Together

Breaking Up to Get Together

I once had a client who was going through a particularly bad divorce. And I mean BAD.

It had been rumbling on for many, many months and was peppered with venomous arguments, disagreements, positions, anger, resentments, the toxic residue from a long-suffering marriage and deep into the blame game.

It was horrible.

Every issue from the past that had been pushed down and overcome for years was now spewing forth like a busted fire hydrant, and it was saturating the already life-heavy discourse over the dog, the house, the cars, the debts, the cash, the kids, the payments, and when collapsed with the all too frequent and unstable flash points over why the marriage failed, who was to blame, who was the more dysfunctional or unwell all the way down the rabbit hole to the nastiest accusations and destruction of character.

Even listening to this client explain their story was exhausting. Now, it would be nice if I could say this was one client in a long career of coaching people through the most troubling phases of their lives, but it was not. I've had many, many clients over the years with very similar circumstances.

The one consistent piece in all of this was the coaching I gave them.

It always began with a simple question, with the only stipulation that their answer had to be to-the-bone honest.

I would ask, "Do you want a divorce, or do you want a divorce that's 'fair'"?

Every single client answered in *exactly* the same way: "I want a divorce that's fair."

And right there lay the battleground for the entire thing. Fair.

Fair to whom? It's little wonder that the final resting place of what is "fair" ends up in a court. Was this just about the even distribution of goods or something else? The kids? We'll get to that.

However, it didn't take much digging to find some treasured nuggets hidden in the background of this "war" as many of those clients began to share that what they really wanted was payback or some kind of emotional revenge for the way they felt they had been treated. This quest for fairness went much farther than evenly splitting the bath towels, coffee mugs, and soon-to-be-expired Target gift cards.

The pain and suffering had to be the same too. Because anything less would seem like the other person got away with it, that they had "won," and if someone wins then obviously some else is the loser, and the thought of building from there, as the defeated or the wronged, seems like just too much to bear.

And so it continued: attack, defend, defend, attack, and on and on and on. The emotional toll was heavy.

How in the hell does someone get out of this mess? Well, it starts by seeing the exit as more important than the exit *your way*. But that is only a beginning.

Let's step back a bit here because at first glance it might seem kind of weird that I'm talking about how to break up when we're knee deep into a relationship book! After all, if you're reading a book of this kind, it probably means you *don't* want your current relationship to end. That's kind of the whole point of reading it.

Either that or you're single and hoping to start a successful relationship in the near future. Successful as in, you know, not ending in a breakup.

So, at this point, you might be thinking something like, *For fuck's sake, Gary, if I was just gonna end it, I could've saved myself some time and not read the rest of the book.*

Maybe you're thinking I've led you on a bit. That I've filled your head with all this BS for the past few chapters, only to turn around and tell you, "Look, I don't think this is going to work out . . ."

I get it. But if you'll give me a chance to explain, you'll realize that thinking about how to break up actually makes logical sense. And no, it doesn't necessarily mean your relationship is going to end. In fact, it'll ultimately make you less likely to break up. Really. Think about it.

What's one of the first things you have to do when you get on an airplane? Don't they tell you all about what you have to do if the thing goes down? Masks will come down from the overhead compartment; affix yours first before helping your child with theirs. A life vest is under your seat; place the vest over your head and pull the cord to inflate. Exits are here, here, and here . . . and so on.

It's basically a whole lecture on how to best survive a crash.

And at no time during the demonstration of buckling your seat belt does anyone stand up and yell, "Why the fuck are you telling us all this?" Okay, maybe a couple of people have done that, before, but those people are the exceptions. Don't be like them.

You're certainly not sitting there, fingers in your ears, eyes closed, screaming "LA, LA, LA, LA, LA, LA!" at the top of your voice because you don't want to interrupt the high of going on your dream vacation with the dark prospect of maybe having to deal with the plane going down.

Maybe you tune the whole thing out and just stare out the window or at your phone, especially if you've already sat through the spiel a few times in the past. But that only further proves my point.

You're on a plane learning how to crash . . . yet you don't assume you're actually going to need that stuff. You're not crashing, right? In fact, you're so comfortable in the thought that it's not going to crash that you might not even be bothered to pay attention at all.

The truth is, when it comes to airplanes, it's true, you likely won't crash. In fact, in the case of that giant metal tube in the sky, chances are you'll never, ever crash, even if you take dozens or even hundreds of flights in your lifetime.

The likelihood of your relationship ending is, statistically, far higher than meeting the ground ahead of schedule in a plane. And yet you are willing to "wing it" if it were to happen. You're also living with that great unknown in the background of your mind, stuffed down in hope, positivity, and denial.

So we're facing a mystery here, we're embracing the possibility of something, no matter how painful the prospect of that may seem to you. We're preparing and being responsible for who we are and who we will be.

You're not learning to break up because you're hoping to break up. You're doing it so you can survive a breakup if it does come. It's a matter of knowing where the emergency exits are and how to hold yourself together in the face of it all.

But if you're already in a relationship? Well, better late than never.

Of course, if you've got some past relationships under your belt, you might be thinking, *HA! I already know how to break up. I've done it before. A lot.*

After all, any idiot can figure out how to end a relationship, right? These days, you don't even have to talk to the person: just text it to them. Or don't say anything and "ghost" them. Just disappear. Admittedly some of that is a lot harder when you're married with three kids, two hamsters, a blind dog, and a subscription for organic wine to think about.

But as with anything, there's a big difference between breaking up the right way and the wrong way. There's a big difference between a breakup that's a complete shit show, leaving toxic resentment and long-term grudges in its wake, and one that's a little more, dare I say, workable, if not even pleasant.

Unfortunately, most of us go about breakups the wrong way.

When Breaking Up Is Hard to Do

In most breakups, we frame them in the context of blame and deal with the entire situation from there. And usually, yes, that blame is on the other person even if it's you who did the "wrong." You'll find a way to turn the event in your favor.

They didn't show me the affection I need. They don't have their shit together. They cheated. They lied. They killed my goldfish. Or they just don't make me feel the way I did when we first met.

Now sure, sometimes your partner really is on the hook for that stuff.

But what happens when we approach breakups with this mindset is we start to lose sight of something. And that something is the person we said we'd be, the way we said we'd act at the beginning of the relationship.

We drag this conversation back to the first few chapters of the book where we talked about vows.

When you got married, you promised to do all kinds of shit, to have and to hold, to love and to cherish, in sickness and in health. Right? You agreed to act a certain way.

And sure, life happens, things go wrong, sometimes very wrong, we want to defend ourselves and protect ourselves to deal with serious issues such as separation and divorce. It's painful and unsettling and scary. So up comes the mechanism for emotional survival.

When once we were loving and cherishing, we now want to hurt and be spiteful. Instead of supporting them, we want to take as much as we can from them, whether it's wounding them about the house, the kids, or whatever other collateral damage gets produced. All's fair in love and war, eh?

No. At least it doesn't have to be that way. You simply don't have to turn yourself into something you have to justify or recuperate from no matter how tempting it may seem in that emotion-blazing moment.

You can still be you. You can still stay true to the things that are important to you.

What if you could leave a relationship in the same way you came into it? In a way that sanctifies your peace of mind, your well-being, and your ability to step into the next phase of your life without the need to completely rebuild who you are, but rather to expand into something truly great instead of starting at the bottom again?

And even though there may be tons of reasons and justifications, that the pain inflicted or the neglect indulged or the selfishness unleashed may leave you feeling you need to defend yourself or strike back, it doesn't have to be that way.

Well, that's how you break up. Look back at those relationship values again. They don't just guide you through how you can create a brilliant relationship, they also can influence who you'll need to be should the day ever come where you or your partner decides this is no longer working. For whatever reason.

I'm not asking you get yourself wrapped up in the specific items of your relationship values (some may be inappropriate to splitting up), but nonetheless I'm inviting you to embrace the *spirit* of who you said you would be.

If you're not married or have no children from your partnership, the stakes are at least a little lower, and the agreement you made getting into the relationship is often less explicit. But it's pretty much the same story.

So what do you take from what I'm laying out here?

This is all about the critical nature of staying true to who you are. It's not like you won't fall off the horse, it's not like life won't get in the way of your biggest plans, but the one thing you can control, the one thing you have a say in is who you will be when life comes calling.

I know there are people who will disagree with what I'm saying, I'm clear there are litanies of counselors and mediators and lawyers and the like who will tell you to fight, fight, fight. and, truth be told, you may need those kinds of folks to help you work some things out should you ever separate; but even then, what I'm saying holds true.

Never abandon who you are because when you are settled about what you value, what is important in the grand scheme of things, your heart and your head are always aligned. You know where the masks are, where the life jackets and exits are, and now you can just let all that be.

An Honorable You

So if you're true to yourself and your values, you can survive anything, even a breakup. Which bring us into the present and your relationship right now.

You're in because you said you're in. This is about you, them, and this thing called your relationship.

Your values are your guide, but if you think that's the whole picture, you're mistaken. They are supposed to influence you, to remind you of what's important, to interrupt those little incompletions, arguments, and the ever-creeping distortions of your job, money situation, family crises, and whatever else you could throw into the blender called your life.

What you make the relationship about has to actually be what it's about. Everything else is just "stuff."

But living life this way makes you a very unique and distinct kind of human being, someone who can successfully overcome constraints and roadblocks, a transcendent power in a society where sacrificing your life and passions to circumstances is the norm.

You become a man or woman of honor.

That's right. Honor. To know yourself as honorable.

I know, it all sounds a bit like *Lord of the Rings*, right? But it isn't in the slightest, it's deadly serious, and trust me when I say it is the foundation to any great accomplishment in your life. In many ways, you could say everything I talk about and write about is to finally have you see the real power in constituting yourself as an honorable human being.

What is honor? If you set aside whatever mental image comes up for you, honor for a human being is acting in a way that aligns with what you say. That there is a certain glue between words and actions even when those words are being questioned by pressure or circumstance or emotion.

That is to say, you treat what you said with the highest regard even when that's difficult!

If you're in a relationship with someone who is just no longer willing to participate in a way that has your lives work, do you just stick with it and pretend it's okay until you die? NO! In fact, that would be living in pretense, and living *that* way has no honor! Pretense is another word for inauthenticity or not genuine. Anything you are pretending is inauthentic, even pretending to be happy.

This is a complete reinvention of self, to begin exploring life, love, success, all of it, as an honorable being. I've had many people ask me why I've managed to accomplish what I have done in this life. and my answer is always the same. Honor. I treat what I say like it's a big fucking deal. And I act accordingly.

Does being someone of honor make you perfect? No.

Will you always get it right? No.

Will you wrestle with much of the same shit you have always done? Probably.

So what's different? You are finally called to BE someone when you operate with honor. You cannot go on being this ordinary, boring, fucking reflection of what it is to be a human being. You have to strive for something greater, something that stretches you and calls you out when you're down, the kind of stuff that gets under your skin and fires up the possibility of something remarkable.

Those values? Get out there, make them fucking real, talk, act, and behave in a way that aligns you with all that stirs your heart. If that looks like bravely and honorably ending a relationship, so be it. If it looks like staying in a relationship and working through the hard parts, that's honorable too.

You don't need help, you need releasing. You're not in need of love, you need to love. Let that shit out, unleash your love on that poor sucker you married. They have no idea what's coming! Look them in the eye and let them know. What the hell, freak them out a bit!

Love like there's no tomorrow, because the straight of it is, there's not. There's only now.

Be obvious. This isn't a game, this is real, your real life; never let anyone in your life be left with the idea that they think you love them. It has to be plain, real, and authentic.

There is no alternative and there is no greater expression of you than being who you said you would be, and that, my friend, is available only when you operate with honor.

An honorable you.

11
Love
the
Struggle

Love the Struggle

This is the point in the book where I wanted to give you something inspiring, something to stir your heart and raise the game of your relationship to propel you to new heights of effectiveness in this area of your life.

Instead, I am opting for you to be grounded with your feet firmly planted in reality rather than floating in a fragile bubble of positivity and hope that would undoubtedly be popped by one nefarious deed or another at some point in the not too distant future.

With that in mind, I'm reminded of a flippant comment that rose to the surface of an otherwise sludgy interaction about what God knows. It jumped at me, invaded my thoughts so much I could not only never forget it but for the life of me cannot even remember who in the hell actually said it.

It went like this—"You have to love the struggle."

WHY!?? gasped my inner critic. After all, isn't the point of life to get *out* of the struggle, to get past it and on to better things? If I love the struggle, doesn't that mean I'm stuck with it forever. I mean, where's the incentive?

However, right then I let myself be with this statement and have since revisited it many, many times over the years since, and it has bailed me out of more bullshit than I care to remember. For those of you who still question the power of words, think again.

So in the context of relationships, what does it mean to love the struggle?

Here's an example. Most of us go to a coffee shop with a fair degree of consistency in our day-to-day lives. Think of your daily haunt and picture it in your mind right now. Imagine yourself opening the door and walking in. Picture the predictable sights, sounds, and smells as you make your way toward the counter where you order.

You've done this lots of times. Maybe you're going in there at a time of day that's typically busier, or you've been thinking ahead of the game and sneaking in before the lines get too big. As you well know, there's a massive difference between 7:02 and 7:08 on a Monday morning.

You also know where almost everything is in there, whether it's the cashier or the pickup point or the display case. It's your place, and there's a certain degree of comfort in that for you. It's actually one of the reasons why franchises do so well; people like them when things are familiar to them. Included in that, are, of course, some of the things that you don't quite like about that place, but overall, it's at the very least good enough for what you require, right?

You don't walk in there grumbling about why your local Starbucks smells like coffee, right? That would be weird. It's a fucking Starbucks! Ehhh . . . duh! And sure, there are those days when the lines are too big, or your coffee just wasn't right, or the cashier took too long, or you forgot your wallet or purse, or they were out of the thing you wanted but next day you're in there as usual. It's no biggie, it's part of the deal sometimes.

Now think about this: have there been any days when you walked in and a giraffe was grazing in the back corner as "Jazztastic," a live twenty-eight-piece New Orleans jazz band, was cranking out their famous Red Hot Chili Peppers musical montage, and the gentle scent of high-grade military rocket fuel terrorized your nostrils?

No, of course not; that stuff just doesn't happen in Starbucks (or anywhere), and if anything like that ever did happen, you'd be shocked to the core. I mean, what the actual hell?! It would be a big deal in an otherwise uneventful day. You'd be talking about if forever! You couldn't ignore it or unimagine it because that kind of stuff is just not supposed to show up in a freaking coffee shop.

The point here is, there's a certain way that place is, it's not always perfect or likely not the most idyllic spot in the universe from time to time, but you like what you like, and that's the deal.

In short, you accept the whole of it for all that it is. Love the struggle.

What Will Be, Will Be

You see, I never fully settled into the idea of entirely loving the struggle. In fact, when I say that, what really springs to mind is that there *will* be struggle. That's right, regardless of what you do, in life there will be those times when it's not ideal, when it's not what you wanted or expected or desired. When your plans are being attacked or dismantled and your peace of mind is under threat.

In coffee shops, there are lines. In coffee shops, they don't always have what you want. In coffee shops, they sometimes get your order wrong. Don't like those things? Fine. So what? It might be annoying, but it's what you're willing to put up with for having someone else make you coffee every morning.

In coffee shops, as in life, it all comes with the territory of whichever situation you find yourself in. It's all part of the deal.

However, unlike putting up with a long line or a wrong order, you don't respond that way in your relationship. You don't shrug your shoulders and say, "Oh well, tomorrow will be better." Your problem in your relationship is that you resist when it's not going your way. You get pissed off or deflated and add whichever inconvenience is rattling your cage to the myriad of other little things you've stashed under your skin. You're like a squirrel hoarding for the winter except you're gathering complaints and incompletions for your relationship. Then you dwell in them, you think about them, you talk about them, you make otherwise insignificant things a bigger deal than they need to be, and then you wonder why things just aren't the way they used to be.

Things aren't the way they used to be because back then, you were creating and living and exploring your relationship, and you took it on because it is what you wanted. It wasn't a burden or a struggle because you weren't looking for love or joy or passion, you *were* those things!

Your relationship is not gonna go your way at times. You will argue, fight, and disagree. You might question your relationship and the point of being in it. You may wonder if your "meant to be" partner is wandering the earth like a lost soul or how you might ever get beyond whichever roadblock is currently in the way. You might be sick of the sound of your partner's voice or their tooth brushing habits or the slurp they make when drinking their almond milk like it's a gift from the gods.

In other words, you will find yourself in a place where petty, inconsequential bullshit seems like the end of the world when really most of what you are dealing with is a pile up of "stuff" that you've never truly accepted either about them, yourself, or what it actually takes to forge a meaningful life with another. All of that stuff can seem hopeless and burdensome because it has replaced what being in a relationship is really all about: creation.

And what you are creating in your relationship comes from the values you are living out of, the commitment to those values, and the vow to hold to those values throughout the relationship.

Relationships are a reflection of what you are up to, of holding your commitments in front of yourself like a beacon, a light shining the way both in the present and into the future. Your commitments, those values you hold so dear, are the templates for all you do. Not feeling it? Do it. Not getting what you thought you would get in return? Do it.

If you value love, commit to taking a loving action, do something that reflects who YOU are.

If you value passion, create passion in your relationship. After all, it's your commitment, right? Do something passionate.

Whatever you are committed to, BE THAT PERSON. Don't apologize for it, dilute it, or bend it in any way. In other words, be the fullest expression of all you are committed to in this union today and today and today and today until you either run out of todays or you are no longer willing to honor that commitment any longer. Both take courage and yes, you guessed it, commitment.

Relationships are about creation, creation, creation. There's nothing else. All of life is relationships, and the quality of those relationships dictates the quality of your life. You are in charge of your own triggers.

You can free yourself from your hooks and empower yourself to create a great relationship.

You are the architect, the magician, the wonder of what it is to be alive, and you have the limitless ability to shift yourself and life itself. You bring yourself to the idea of "us" instead of the ordinary and everyday game that everyone else is playing, the game of "me."

You can't be in an "us" if your first concern is "me," but similarly it doesn't work if you only make it about "them" either. You have to be the champion for this union. Us.

Right now, get yourself present to your commitments. Who are they demanding you show up as? Don't just sit there hopeless; wake up, show up. Show up for yourself and what's possible between you and your partner. No more mindless complaining about problems; you can be the solution. No more blame, shame, and guilting; that shit has no place in a loving and substantial relationship. In short, give a fuck. Be honest with yourself and your partner, be authentic with nothing to hide, and play full out like your happiness depends on it because you and I both know it really does.

Every day is an opportunity for you to create from your own commitments, to build your day, your week, your vacations, your downtime, your down-in-the-dirt, nitty-gritty of a life from the kind of values that inspire you, and if there ever comes a day when you're no longer inspired by them, create some new ones!

A real, loving, knock-your-socks-off relationship is something you can have. I have full faith in your ability to create it and sustain it. No matter what your relationship status is at this moment, allow yourself to be shaped by a different kind of living where your commitments inform and direct what you do with your everyday thoughts, feelings, and actions. Where you are a person guided by values and the power of your words, not your emotions. Where you become a loving, honorable person.

Get out there, be love, be connection, be us. Love the struggle even when it *is* a struggle. It's worth it in the end.

You are worth it, your life is worth it. Get out of the ordinary, reach for the extraordinary, live like a miracle with nothing left out and all you got thrown into it.

It's all a fucking game anyway.

Get in there.

About the Author

Born and raised in Glasgow, Scotland, Gary moved to the United States in 1997. This opened up his pathway to the world of personal development, specifically to his love of ontology and phenomenology. This approach, in which he rigorously trained for a number of years, saw him rise to become a senior program director with one of the world's leading personal development companies. After years of facilitating programs for thousands of people all over the world and later studying and being influenced by the philosophies of Martin Heidegger, Hans-Georg Gadamer, and Edmund Husserl, Gary is producing his own brand of "urban philosophy." His lifelong commitment to shifting people's ability to exert real change in their lives drives him each and every day. He has a no-frills, no-bullshit approach that has brought him an ever-increasing following drawn to the simplicity and real-world use of his work.

A few more words of wisdom . . .

Available wherever books, ebooks, and audiobooks are sold.